FAMOUS SINGLES OF THE BIBLE

Brian L. Harbour

D0675422

BROADMAN PRESS
Nashville, Tennessee 37234

To my parents
Brunie and Imogene,
who provided a firm foundation
of faith in God and love for the truth
upon which to build my life

© Copyright 1980. Broadman Press
All rights reserved.

4256-40
ISBN: 0-8054-5640-6

Dewey Decimal Classification: 220.92
Subject headings: BIBLE—BIOGRAPHY // SINGLE PERSONS

Library of Congress Catalog Card Number: 79-56309

Printed in the United States of America

Preface

What is a family? A mother and father and two children? Sometimes, but not always. *Family* does not equal *couple* any more, for more and more households are headed by singles. With no-fault divorce, changing attitudes toward divorce, and growing acceptance of singleness as a viable life-style, many people are opting to face life unmarried.

This is a book for the growing number of singles in the land and for those who love them. It has grown out of my experiences with single adults in the churches I have pastored and out of my attempts to minister to them. I have tried to make the book thoroughly biblical by basing the discussions on characters who are introduced to us in the Word of God. From these experiences of yesterday, I have sought to extract truths which are relevant today.

Singleness was not a common life-style in Bible times; most people were married. Nevertheless, sprinkled throughout the Scriptures are cameos of men and women who, either by choice or circumstance, spent some time in the single state. There were those who never married, like John the Baptist, as well as those like Naomi and Vashti who, through the death or divorce of a mate, entered the realm of the formerly married. As you read the book perhaps you will see your life projected in one of the lives of these famous singles of the Bible.

I want to say a special word of thanks to the singles of

the Shiloh Terrace Baptist Church in Dallas, Texas, and the First Baptist Church in Pensacola, Florida, who have so greatly influenced my life. From them I have learned the questions singles are asking. In their lives, I also have seen demonstrated some exciting answers to those questions.

I want to express my deep appreciation to my outstanding secretary, Nelma Camp, who so carefully and expertly typed this manuscript.

Thanks also goes to my wife, Jan, who allowed me the extra hours at night that were necessary to complete this book.

Brian L. Harbour
Pensacola, Florida

Contents

1
The Shunned Single: *Hagar*
Genesis 21

The boy who greeted me at the door had a bright smile and a handsome face. Peeping out from behind him were two other children, both as attractive as he. The family had visited our church as prospects, and I was following up on their visit. Although the parents were not at home, my first impression of the family was a good one. That impression was confirmed as I later visited with the parents. They spoke of their past involvement in church. They shared with me an intense desire to find a church that would feed them spiritually and provide an active program for their children. Not long afterward, the entire family joined our church. They seemed to be a delightful family.

Months passed during which the family planted themselves firmly in the life of our church. Because it was a large church, I had little personal contact with them for a while. I knew they were there and thought they were happy.

Then one afternoon the wife made an appointment to come by for a chat. I thought perhaps she wanted to find some ways in which her family could become more involved in the ministries of the church. When she walked into my office I was shocked. Her face was tight and drawn. Her eyes, covered by dark glasses, bore evidence of continuous crying. She had lost twenty or thirty pounds. She was only a shadow of her former self. Gone was the joy and excitement that had so characterized her when I first met her several months before.

What had gone wrong? The story was a familiar one. "My husband has been having an affair," she blurted out as soon as she sat down. "He says he is in love with another woman and wants a divorce. He doesn't love me anymore."

Why does this happen? Why would a man who had invested over fifteen years in a marriage suddenly throw it all away for an office romance? His explanation reflects on our times. "Everybody is doing it," is what he told her. His wife's explanation was more pointed: "He has rejected me. He chose someone else instead of me." She was tossed aside, rejected, shunned!

That this is not simply a modern-day phenomenon becomes evident as we read the story of Hagar. She was the victim of another woman's jealousy and of a man too weak to stand up for the right. She, too, like her modern-day counterparts, was tossed aside for another.

The background of the story is found in the book of Genesis. Abraham, the one who was called "a friend of God," had been chosen to father God's special people. Promises were made of a vast inheritance and a lineage so numerous they could not even be counted. According to the promises, Abraham was to be the father of a great nation.

There was a problem, however. Abraham was eighty-six years old and his wife Sarah was seventy-six. And they did not have any children. How would all of God's marvelous promises be fulfilled without a child? At their ages, they were beginning to get a little concerned.

A custom of the day seemed to offer a way out. It was acceptable in that age for a childless woman to offer her maid to her husband. If the maid bore a child, the child would be accepted in the same status as a son born of the wife. So Sarah sent Hagar, her handmaid, to sleep with

Abraham. The plan worked. Hagar conceived. A child was to be born of Abraham, so now God's promises could be fulfilled.

That's when the fireworks began. Construct a tempestuous triangle between two women and one man and then watch the sparks fly. One boy asked his father why the law prohibited a man from marrying two women. The father replied, "It is the government's way of protecting those who cannot protect themselves!"

Two women and one man is one woman too many. Jealous of the fact that Hagar was to produce a child for Abraham, Sarah confronted her husband with a choice. "It is either me or her. You've got to make a decision." In any triangle a choice will inevitably be made and the ax will fall on the third party. This is what happened to Hagar. It continues to happen to millions of modern-day Hagars like the one with whose story I began the chapter. Let's use Hagar's experience to discover some insights for the shunned singles of today.

THE REJECTION

Hagar was involuntarily pulled into the relationship with Abraham and Sarah. Then, because of Sarah's jealousy, she was just as rudely excluded. The hurt was shattering. The Bible pictures Hagar in the desert, having been cast off and rejected. She put her son under a bush. Then she sat down and wept "about a bowshot away" (Gen. 21:16). This common Hebrew idiom meant "as far off as archers customarily put their target." Whether Hagar did that to prevent her son from seeing her cry or to avoid watching her son die, the point is the same. Rejection had created an intense hurt in her heart which overflowed in tears and anguish.

On the way to a funeral one day, the man with whom I rode mentioned his recent divorce. He thought he and his wife had a good relationship. This illusion was shattered by the discovery that his wife had a secret lover. Divorce soon followed. When I asked him how he reacted to the divorce, he answered, "Mainly, I was hurt. It was like a fire which burned in the pit of my stomach and then moved out to my extremities."

Probably no other experience causes the degree of hurt that comes when the one you love rejects you. This emotional earthquake expresses itself in a variety of ways.

Sometimes *guilt* is the result. "If only I had treated him better," is the way it is usually expressed. One young lady whose husband had left her told me, "I knew he liked to go out at night. But I was just too tired. I always had some excuse. I just wasn't very much fun to be with."

To deal with guilt, one must first analyze the feeling to determine whether it is true guilt or false guilt. False guilt is a feeling which has no foundation in fact. When close examination reveals that there is no reason to feel guilty, that you gave it your best, and that the circumstances which led to the rejection were really beyond your control, then the guilt can be released. When the guilt is determined to be true, then one must follow the biblical pattern which leads to forgiveness: confession and restitution which lead to changed actions. The promise of God's Word is, "If we confess our sins, He is faithful and righteous to forgive us our sins and to cleanse us from all unrighteousness" (1 John 1:9).

Another emotional manifestation following rejection is *anger*. "How could he have done this to me?" One woman I knew filled the role of a "scholarship wife:" She put her husband through school. Shortly after he was established in his new job, he began a relationship with another woman. The rejected wife's initial statement to me when she came for counseling was, "It just isn't fair. I worked my fingers to the bone putting him through school. Now he has just tossed me aside." Anger was the result.

Anger is certainly understandable in such an experience. The trouble with anger is that it has a double edge. Anger can cause more damage to the person who harbors it than to the one to whom the anger is directed. The writer of Proverbs said, "He who digs a pit will fall into it,/And he who rolls a stone, it will come back on him" (Prov. 26:27).

Anger can actually lead to physical ailments. One doctor described a college student who had severe stomach pains. Investigation revealed that the source of the pains was a bitter resentment against some men who had defrauded his grandfather many years before. His anger led to such severe abdominal distress that he was not able to maintain good enough grades to stay in school.

This same doctor cited a hospital study in which resentment was the most prominent personality characteristic in 96 percent of the patients suffering from colitis. Resentment is nothing more than smoldering anger. Since personal resentment can also be directly related to toxic goiters, fatal heart attacks, and circulatory problems, this doctor concluded that it might be accurately written on thousands of death certificates that the victim died of "grudgitis."[1]

I remember an incident on the old "Amos and Andy Show" that clearly illustrates the two-edged destructiveness of anger. Andy annoyed Kingfish by constantly slapping him on the back. Every time Andy saw Kingfish he would rap him between the shoulders. Fed up, Kingfish devised a plan to vent his anger. With one of his copyrighted smiles on his face, the Kingfish told Amos, "I've got a plan to get even with Andy. I've strapped this dynamite on my back and the next time he slaps me on the back, it will blow his hand off!'' (Not to mention King-fish's back.)

Rejection also leads to *ego-deflation*. "If she can take him away from me, then I must not be much." For over a year I counseled with one lady who was a classic illustration of this rejection. Previously a vivacious, outgoing woman, her husband's rejection sent her into a tailspin. Months passed before she was able to believe in herself again.

Some psychologists call adultery a "psychic injury." It pierces to the very soul. Rejection, which in its ultimate form is adultery, inevitably carries with it the connotation that you are less appealing or attractive than the other person.

What is the answer for this psychic trauma? How can the ego be built up again? The truth of God's Word is helpful at this point. The good news of Christ is that every individual is of ultimate worth and value to God. "But as many as received Him, to them He gave the right to be-come children of God" (John 1:12). "No longer do I call you slaves; for the slave does not know what his master is doing; but I have called you friends, for all things that I have heard from My Father I have made known to you" (John 15:15). "And so we should not be like cringing, fearful slaves, but we should behave like God's very own children, . . . For his Holy Spirit speaks to us deep in our hearts, and tells us that we really are God's children" (Rom. 8:15-16, TLB). Our value and self-worth is not determined by the acceptance or rejection of our fellow-men, not even by the acceptance or rejection of a mate. Our worth is rooted in the declaration that we are children of God!

Time will also help. One lady, having gone through the trauma of ego-deflation, made a startling discovery.

Something good actually came out of her divorce. "The best thing that's happened," she said, "is that someone I knew only slightly emerged as a good and true friend, a strong but compassionate, funny, articulate person whom I am beginning to enjoy thoroughly. That person is me!"[2]

Perhaps the most damaging emotional aftereffect of rejection is *loneliness.* "I can't stand the nighttime hours without her," is the way one young man put it. This is the loneliness that comes from being alone. But it goes even deeper than that. One divorcee was asked what she missed most about her former marital relationship. She answered, "I miss the expectancy when someone you care about is going to call or come home."

One writer distinguishes between *physical loneliness* and *psychological loneliness.* Physical loneliness is the fact that there is no one with you in the house. You are alone at the dinner table, alone in the den at the end of a day, alone in the bed. That is physical loneliness. Psychological loneliness is the feeling of being alone in life. No one is there to share your triumphs or help you bear your trials. The direction of your life has to be determined by you alone. That's psychological loneliness.[3]

Rejection usually confronts the shunned single with both types of loneliness. Vital to survival is a healthy means of dealing with loneliness.

Often those who are single again try to avoid facing the reality of their aloneness. One young man told me that for three months after his divorce he almost killed himself with endless activity. He could not stay at home; he was always on the go.

Others cope with the loneliness by immediately initiating a new relationship. Although hurt by the rejection of their former mates, they soon find others. Two-thirds of the women who are divorced and three-fourths of the men will marry again. The paradox of this is expressed by the woman who said, "All men are selfish, brutal, and inconsiderate; and I wish I could find one!"

Why do so many shunned singles soon become part of a couple again? One reason is the awesome loneliness that their rejection has caused.

The loneliness of rejection is best handled by filling your time with worthwhile activities, properly spaced to give time for rest and relaxation. Developing platonic relationships can help fill the void of aloneness temporarily without prematurely entering into a new permanent relationship for which you are not emotionally ready. One single again said, "I've spent many a day alone, but never a lonely day."[4] That can happen when the loneliness of rejection is properly handled.

Ultimately, the rejected mate will experience *depression*. "There is nothing left for me to live for. I'm just going to give it all up." This is where rejection ultimately led Hagar. The anger, ego-deflation, and loneliness were swallowed up in a deep depression which robbed her of any further desire to live.

If that is where your rejection has led you, then hold on for a moment. Let's see what happened to Hagar.

THE RESOURCES

As Hagar lifted her voice and wept (Gen. 21:16), her eyes were suddenly opened to some resources that were available to her. She didn't see them at first. The shock was too traumatic. She had eyes but could not see. Gradually, however, she came to the point where, with open eyes, she was able to recognize some sources of help.

When you have been shunned, even when the emotional aftermath involves guilt, anger, loneliness, and depression, there are some resources around you in which you can find assistance.

You can perhaps find help in your *family*. Notice that

the voice of young Ishmael brought a response from God. Hagar discovered that she was not alone in the crisis. Her son was with her. The strength of a family member pulled her back from the edge of depression.

When rejection comes, the loving context of family members who care can provide an environment for healing and restoration.

Your *friends* can be another source of help. Someone has said that a friend is a person who steps in when the whole world steps out. By reestablishing or developing relationships with friends, the loneliness can be combated, the feeling of self-worth can be restored, and the bitterness can be slowly removed.

The *future* itself is an ally. Time has a healing effect. Just as the passing of time heals a physical wound, the passing of time can also bring healing to the psychic wound caused by rejection. After going through the trauma of rejection and divorce, a group of divorced women were asked to evaluate their status. Eighty-eight percent concluded that their lives were better than when they had been married.[5] Their earlier evaluation at the time of divorce was much gloomier. Time had made a difference.

Another resource is our *heavenly Father.* Earlier in the wilderness, Hagar had turned to God and discovered him to be "the God who sees" (Gen. 16:13). That great truth about God had been forgotten in the shuffle of her activities. In the wilderness again, the truth came to mind once more, so she called on God. When she did she saw what she had not seen before, a well of water from which to fill up a bottle to give to her son (Gen. 21:19).

That is more than merely a factual part of Hagar's experience. It is a paradigm of our experience today. Rejection evolves from guilt to depression because our focus is on ourselves. From that perspective, there does not seem to be any way out of our dilemma. However, when we dare to focus on God, our perspective changes. Now we can see what we did not see before, a well of water in God from whose stream we can be spiritually revived.

When rejection comes, resources for renewal are all around if we but have the eyes to see.

THE RESPONSIBILITY

Another insight into Hagar's recovery was the re-awakened responsibility for her son. God told her that his plans included an outstanding future for her son. Her responsibility was to prepare him for that future. "Hold Ishmael fast," God told her, "for his future is in your hands" (Gen. 21:18, author's paraphrase).

When rejection comes with its emotional earthquake, an inward focus will lead to depression. An outward look, on the other hand, will not only reveal resources previously hidden but will also remind us of responsibilities which we alone can assume.

When you are rejected, your life is not over nor do your responsibilities end. Do you have children? They are your responsibility. Hold them up, for their future is in your hands. Do you have a job? Then commit yourself to it with new fervor. Do you have a house that needs to be cared for? Then direct your creativity toward that task.

Even if you have none of the above, you still have yourself. You are not responsible for everything that happens to you in life. However, you and you alone are responsible for how you react to the things that happen to you.

Rejection does not remove responsibility. It did not for Hagar, neither does it for you. A reminder of her responsibility by God was one of the steps which led to recovery for Hagar. No longer did she have time for self-pity. She had a job to do. With renewed vigor she committed herself to the care of her son.

Lift up your eyes and look beyond yourself. You will not only discover resources to assist you but you will also discover responsibilities to assume.

THE RESULT

The end of the story is only alluded to in the Bible, but it is enough to show us that Hagar recovered beautifully from her rejection. Ishmael did become the father of a great nation. The promises of God were fulfilled. Hagar's life was blessed as she moved in obedience to the plan of God.

A couple of traditions reaffirm the importance of Hagar's life. One tradition suggests that after Sarah died, Hagar became Abraham's wife. If so, Hagar was no longer just a rejected handmaid, she became the respected wife.

Another tradition emphasizes the fact that Ishmael was the ancestor of Mohammed, the dynamic Islamic leader. The strength of Islam, according to this tradition, is said to be bound up with the name of Hagar.[6]

If those traditions are true, then their descriptions of Hagar is a world of difference from the description of Hagar in Genesis 21 when, rejected by Abraham, she was ready to die. She worked through her rejection to regain respect from herself and others.

Are you a shunned single? Have you been tossed aside for another? Don't give up. The final score is not yet in. If you can work through the emotional trauma that rejection causes, if you can lift up your eyes to see the resources that are all around, if you can accept responsibility for your life, then you too can find as Hagar did, the dawning of a new day.

2
The Secular Single: *Deborah*
Genesis 24:59; 35:8

I noticed recently a list of rules for white-collar workers posted in 1872 by a carriage manufacturing company in New York. Among the suggestions were the following: (1) Each clerk will bring a bucket of water and a scuttle of coal for the day's business. (2) Make your pens carefully. You may whittle nibs to your individual taste. (3) Men employees will be given one evening off each week for courting purposes, or two evenings if they go to church regularly. (4) After thirteen hours of labor in the office the employee should spend the remaining time reading the Bible and other good books. (5) The employee who has performed his labor faithfully and without fault for five years will be given an increase of $.05 per day in his pay (providing profits for the business permit).[1]

We've come a long way since then. Working conditions have improved. Hours have been shortened. Pay has increased. We don't even have to whittle our own nibs anymore! Rather than a drudgery to be despised, to many people work is the facet of their lives in which they experience their deepest joy.

One single woman who recently went through a broken romance told me, "I am being affirmed by my work." The secular realm provided a sense of fulfillment in her life.

Embedded in the narrative in Genesis about Rebekah, we find a concise cameo of an ancient counterpart to some single women of today. Deborah was her name. She never had a family of her own. Instead, she found fulfillment in her work.

Deborah was Rebekah's nurse who had come with her from Mesopotamia to the land of Canaan. Afterward, she served faithfully in the family of Jacob and Rachel. This nurse who served the family for two generations was evidently held in great reverence by the family as the story of her burial implies (Gen. 35:8). In early patriarchal families, old nurses like Deborah were often honored as foster-mothers. Although Deborah is only briefly mentioned in the Scriptures, her presence reminds us that the secular realm of work can be a source of fulfillment for the single adult.

THE POSSIBILITIES

A father returned home one evening to find his son with a black eye. He was dismayed to discover that the black eye was a souvenir awarded his son by a girl. "Do you mean," the irate father shouted, "that you were beaten up by a mere girl."

To which the boy replied, "Dad, little girls aren't as mere as they used to be!"

Neither are singles. To be "merely a single" is no longer a barrier that will keep you out of the marketplace or relegate you to a low-income position. Bank of America economist Eric Thor has said, "Singles have become increasingly important in the marketplace."[2]

Evidence of this is seen in the increasing buying power of singles. In 1977, 17 percent of all home buyers were single and 25 percent of all new car purchasers were single. At Lexington Village, a development of Coachhouse Condominiums outside of Chicago, 50 percent of the sales were to professionals who are single. Single people purchased 80 percent of the units in a development of four-plexes in the San Francisco suburb of Fremont. These percentages are being duplicated all over the United States.[3]

Another evidence of an increasing financial base for singles is the advertisement focus on singles. The single hamburger cooker, miniature deep fryers, single hot dog steamers, soup for one, and half-cartons of eggs are some examples of the merchandise that is being geared toward the needs of singles. Merchandisers recognize a blossoming market, and they want to take advantage of it.

Opportunities for single women in the job market are also on the increase. The number of women workers jumped from 25.4 million to 33.3 million from 1964 to 1972. The numbers are expected to increase to 39.2 million by 1980.

In the professions, women are moving up as well. Women are now 41 percent of the work force, and one out of six of them is in a profession. Twenty-four percent of the nation's medical students are women. Twenty-eight percent of all law students are women. Ten times as many women are studying engineering now as in 1970.[4]

Most statistics on women at work do not distinguish between single and married women, thus making a definite evaluation impossible. Nevertheless, it is clear that of the growing number of women in business, a large proportion are single. Single women are, thus, an important part of the movement by women to gain equality in the world of work.

Single women are working more, holding better jobs, receiving higher wages, and liking it. One study of unmarried, professional women revealed that 90 percent were satisfied with their work.[5] Another study of divorced women indicated that two-thirds of the women surveyed saw their work as a career, not just a job. They added that they would continue to work even if they didn't have to.[6]

The possibilities for a single, man or woman, to find

satisfaction in a secular profession seem brighter today than ever before.

THE PROBLEMS

This is not to imply that there are no longer any problems for the single in the secular world. Many problems abound. Of these, two areas deserve special mention.

The first problem area relates to *competition.* Do singles get a fair shake in the move up the corporation ladder? Are they paid on an equal basis with those who are married?

Many singles think that discrimination on the job is a reality. In one survey, 30 percent of the single men and women gave an affirmative answer to the question, "Have you experienced discrimination because you are a single?"

This discrimination shows up also from the side of the employer. A study concerning the relationship of fifty major corporations with singles is indicative. When asked if marriage was an essential to upward mobility, 80 percent of the corporations replied in the negative. However, a majority of the fifty corporations reported that only 2 percent of their executives, including junior management, were single. Sixty percent of the corporations reported that single executives tended to make snap judgments. Twenty-five percent believed singles are less stable than marrieds. Discrimination was very real, although the corporations would not admit it.[8]

This discrimination is usually based on the assumption of a corporation that married people are better investments in terms of responsibility, dependability, and staying power. These attitudes will gradually be changed by the increased numbers of singles on the executive and professional level. The fact that many people are opting for singleness as their permanent life-style, not a temporary status while they are waiting to get married, will also help. Equality will come when a single does not have to be exceptional to make it, when an individual is evaluated strictly on his or her ability rather than on marital status.

The Hawthorne effect will also come into play. The Hawthorne effect received its name from a series of experiments performed at Western Electric's Hawthorne, Illinois, plant from 1924 to 1932. The term means that attention will result in improved performance.[9] An increased emphasis on and attention to singles will result in improved performance by singles. Gradually, the inequities will evaporate.

Contact is another area of problems for singles that relates specifically to single women. The contact between men and women at work often opens up the temptation for sexual involvement. How big a problem is sexual harrassment at work? Very big, according to most sources. A CBS news report on October 23, 1979, concluded that 40 to 70 percent of the women in government jobs surveyed have had to face the reality of sexual harassment on their job.

Part of the explanation of the problem is expressed in this way. "The weaker sex is really the stronger sex because of the weakness of the stronger sex for the weaker sex." As long as the Playboy philosophy prevails in society and permeates our lives, the weakness of the stronger sex for the weaker sex will be there.

What is the solution? As awareness of the problem grows, the legal protection against such harassment will become more effective. In the meantime, care must be taken to avoid being caught in compromising situations. Attention must also be given not to communicate a false impression to the people with whom one works.

Deborah, too, had some problems as a single. Born as a slave, she knew she would spend her life in service to another person. Freedom was something she could only dream about. She had no family and, in reality, no life of her own. Instead of allowing her problems to destroy her, however, she turned all of her creativity and energy loose in her ministry of caring. She found fulfillment in her work.

THE PRINCIPLES

How can that happen to you? How can you, as a secular single, overcome the problems and actualize the potential that God has planted within you?

A good biblical answer to that question is found in 2 Thessalonians 3:6-13.

> Now we command you, brethren, in the name of our Lord Jesus Christ, that you keep aloof from every brother who leads an unruly life and not according to the tradition which you received from us. For you yourselves know how you ought to follow our example, because we did not act in an undisciplined manner among you, nor did we eat anyone's bread without paying for it, but with labor and hardship we kept working night and day so that we might not be a burden to any of you; not because we do not have the right to this, but in order to offer ourselves as a model for you, that you might follow our example. For even when we were with you, we used to give you this order; if anyone will not work, neither let him eat. For we hear that some among you are leading an undisciplined life, doing no work at all, but acting like busybodies. Now such persons we command and exhort in the Lord Jesus Christ to work in quiet fashion and eat their own bread. But as for you, brethren, do not grow weary of doing good.

Three principles emerge from this passage which will lead to fulfillment as a secular single.

First, Paul said we are to work with *commitment*. There are two motivations for work. Compulsion is when you do what you have to do. Commitment is when you do what you want to do. Paul suggested that commitment is the proper motivation. Commitment is not so much a matter of our action as it is a matter of our attitude. An attitude of commitment is the key.

Harry Emerson Fosdick, one of America's greatest preachers of this century, told of a time when his mother sent him to pick a quart of raspberries. He was annoyed because he didn't want to do it. He was in the middle of a game with his friends. The call to work was not a welcome interruption. He reluctantly dragged himself to the berry patch. He chafed under the authority of his mother, as people today chafe under the authority of their bosses. Consequently, he was having a miserable time. Then an idea flashed through his mind. What fun it would be to surprise his mother and pick two quarts of raspberries instead of one. Rather than drudgery, his work now became a challenge. The task was the same, but the attitude was different. It was no longer compulsion. Now it was commitment.

That's the attitude the Bible tells us to take toward our work. The writer of Ecclesiastes says that man is to "take pleasure in all his toil" (3:13, RSV). Deuteronomy 12:18 says, "You shall rejoice before the Lord your God in all your undertakings." In Ecclesiastes the biblical writer says, "Whatever your hand finds to do, verily, do it with all your might" (9:10). "Commit your works to the Lord," suggests the writer of Proverbs, "And your plans will be established" (16:3).

Our biggest need today is not to develop a Christian philosophy of leisure but to develop a Christian philosophy of labor. That begins with a sense of commitment to our job.

Saint Anthony was a devout man who sought to be the best that God wanted him to be. He learned one day of another man who was more righteous than he. Anthony wanted to know the man's secret so that he could apply it to his own life, so he set out in search of the man. He came finally to a certain cobbler named Conrad. Anthony told Conrad that he understood he was the most righteous man in the world. He wanted to know what he did that made him so righteous. Conrad humbly remonstrated concerning his goodness. But he went on to say, "If you wish to know what I do, I don't mind telling you. I mend shoes for a living, and I mend every pair as if I were mending them for Jesus." [10]

Commitment means that we do our work as if we were doing it for Jesus. That attitude will lead to fulfillment.

Second, Paul said we are to work with *cooperation*. In two places in the passage quoted above, Paul mentioned those who live unruly or disorderly lives. The Greek word Paul used was a military word that carried the connotation of marching out of ranks. The picture is of a group of people trying to move with precision but being unable to do so because someone is not cooperating.

Never having been in the military I cannot identify with that. The closest thing in my own experience was my high school band. Often we would march in a parade. Not one line would be straight. We looked like waves of lasagna. Rather than being a band which marched with crisp precision, we looked like an accident seeking a place to happen. Why? Because we marched out of ranks. We didn't cooperate. We weren't in step.

Paul added to his imagery with a play on words in verse 11. Literally, what he said was that the people were busy being busybodies. Instead of busily doing their work, they were busy being busybodies who interfered with other people's work. They were like the wife who, after talking for thirty minutes, said to the marriage counselor, "That's my side of the story. Now, let me tell you his!"

How does this relate to the secular singles of today? Let's apply it. Already we have mentioned the problems that confront the single at work. Sometimes the problems are magnified by an uncooperative spirit on the part of the single.

There are times, of course, when a single will be asked to do things that a Christian should not do, and the Christian image must be maintained. But it is as important to our images as Christians to be known as people who are easy to get along with as it is to be known as people who do not drink, smoke, cuss, or chew and refuse to associate with those that do. Paul said that the Christian is not one who causes problems at work, not a busybody, but one who marches in rank so that the organization can move forward with precision.

If you have problems at work, they might not be because you are discriminated against as a single. The problems may not be because you are a Christian who is suffering for Jesus. The problems might be because you have a rotten personality. They might be because you are busy being a busybody, marching out of rank. The problems might be because you don't try to get along. Instead of criticizing your co-workers or complaining about your conditions, maybe what you need to do is to convert your behavior into the cooperative, quiet spirit that Paul suggested in the Thessalonian letter.

Third, Paul said that we should work with *consistency.* "Do not grow weary of doing good," was his suggestion. The word translated "doing good" carries with it the idea of that which is of high quality. Perhaps the greatest problem at work for all of us, married and single alike, is not that we don't have commitment, not that we don't cooperate, but that we don't consistently do our best. We just do enough to get by.

When young Tom was fired from his job, a friend of his

applied for his position. He said to Tom's boss, "I am applying for the vacancy that Tom left." The boss replied, "Tom didn't leave any vacancy." If you were missing from the job, would there be a vacancy?

A sense of fulfillment comes to us, regardless of how other people evaluate us, if we ourselves know that we have done our very best.

Deborah's worth was appreciated by others. When she died, Jacob buried her under an oak tree near Bethel and named it "the oak of weeping." So deeply did the family appreciate her work that when she died, a great emptiness was felt in their lives. Her greatest sense of fulfillment, however, did not come because of the eulogy at her death but because of the conviction within that she had done her very best.

CONCLUSION

A man was asked the secret for his phenomenal success during his lifetime. "I owe it all to luck," he said. "I had the good luck of liking hard work!" I hope you have that same luck. Then you, like Deborah, can find fulfillment as a secular single.

3
The Selective Single: *Isaac*
Genesis 24—25

Picture a young lady visiting church one day. At twenty-two she has just graduated from college and is beginning a nursing career. An older lady introduces herself to the girl and asks about her husband and children. "I don't have a family," the young nurse answers. "I'm single." "Oh," comes the response, "why is a nice girl like you not married?"

That question is being asked often enough today. It could also have been asked of a selective single of yesteryear named Isaac whose story is found in Genesis 24—25. Isaac was forty years old and still not married (Gen. 25:20). That condition is enough to cause cardiac arrest in some individuals. One woman, desperate at thirty-five, prayed each night, "Lord, it's not just for me. But please send my mother a son-in-law!"

Isaac was certainly a suitable suitor. He was the son of Abraham. He was from good stock, from a family socially respected, and was financially solid. He had a deep religious faith and a healthy respect for his family.

Why was Isaac forty and still single? Because he chose to be. There were no women in the area whom he considered suitable to be his bride. The religious and moral convictions of those who lived in the area did not correlate with the religious and moral convictions that were a part of his life.

Someone has said that the key to happiness in marriage is not so much to find the one person who will make you happy as it is to avoid the ones who will make you miserable. Isaac had succeeded in avoiding those candidates who would have made him miserable.

Underlying the choice by Isaac and his father (for the choice was partially Abraham's according to the custom of the day) for Isaac to remain single was the conviction that whom you marry is an extremely important matter. In the words of the traditional Episcopal marriage ceremony, marriage is not "to be entered into unadvisedly or lightly; but reverently, discreetly, advisedly, and in the fear of God."[1] Because of the significance and solemnity of marriage, you need to be selective about whom you marry.

For those of you to whom marriage is a future possibility instead of a present reality, I want to share with you what it will take to be a selective single.

PROGRESS AT THE RIGHT RATE

To be a selective single, first of all, means to progress at the right rate.

A couple with serious marital problems came to me for counseling about three years ago. I asked them how they met. The husband told me that he was painting a church one day. He looked over into a yard next door and saw a girl sunbathing in her swimsuit. He said to his co-worker, "I think I'm in love." Putting down his brush, he went over to meet the girl. Two weeks later they were married!

That, my friends, is too fast. Much greater are the possibilities for success when you dare to progress at the right rate. I believe that Abraham kept a close eye on Isaac to measure his development. When he felt that Isaac was mature enough, Abraham put in motion the steps that eventuated in Isaac's marriage.

In our day, we have a tool to help us progress at the right rate. It is called the dating game. Dating serves the purpose today of developing an individual interpersonally and preparing him or her for marriage. It is of vital importance in our American style of living, for we live in a diverse society. There is no standardized method of child rearing in America today. Areas of the country, local traditions, ethnic peculiarities—all of these add up to a varied standard of child rearing.

How does dating help? It allows individuals from diverse backgrounds to test their emotional and psychological compatibility. It exposes an individual to all kinds of personality types and gives him a chance to learn what kind of person he enjoys being with the most. It also helps a person develop interpersonal skills that will be invaluable in the marriage relationship.

Dating, therefore, is a tool that enables a proper rate of progression. This proper rate of progression is often short-circuited by the tendency toward "going steady."

Why do young people go steady? Usually, there are two reasons. One is *status.* There is something ego-satisfying about having your own girl or guy. Another benefit of going steady is *security.* You don't have to worry about who you'll take to the game or to the prom. You've got it all sewed up. That's security.

These benefits, however, are overshadowed by the dangers. Going steady prevents your exposure to a number of different types of people and thus limits your understanding of what a satisfactory marriage partner would be like.

Even more dangerous is the temptation to premature intimacy that going steady encourages. To paraphrase a well-known saying, "Familiarity breeds consent!" Often, forced marriages are the result. The latest census bureau report shows that one fourth of all newlywed women from 1972-1976 under the age of twenty-five either had a child before marriage or were pregnant when they arrived at the altar.[2] Another study revealed that the divorce rate was twice as high among couples whose marriage took place after a premarital pregnancy than those not faced with a premarital pregnancy.[3]

Even when pregnancy is not involved, teenage marriages are more likely to fail because the individuals have not yet developed their own identities. They are not yet secure enough about who they are to be able to give themselves to another person.

Don't cut the dating game short by a premature marriage. Use the dating game to learn about other people and to learn about yourself. Success in marriage will only come when two people are sufficiently informed to know what they are doing, and sufficiently mature to be able to do it.[4] And that takes time. A selective single is one who progresses at the right rate.

USE THE RIGHT BAIT

To be a selective single you need also to use the right bait.

A couple was fighting one day. The wife said to the husband, "You were not the only fish in the sea, you know."

"That may be true," he responded, "but I can tell you there was better bait too."

Another newlywed said to his wife on their first night back from the honeymoon, "Dear, I hope you don't mind if I point out a few of your faults I have noticed."

"That's quite all right," she replied with feigned sweetness, "it was those faults that kept me from getting a better husband."

Look at yourself. Are you a person who anyone would want to marry? If you are fishing for a mate, what about your bait?

Isaac was a man who had been taught by his father the importance of faith and hard work. He built on that foundation through his own personal devotion to God. He prepared himself for marriage so that when the opportunity arose, he was ready.

How about you?

What kind of physical shape are you in? Do you take care of yourself physically? Are you clean and neat? Do you eat right? Do you try to be as attractive as you can be? Someone has suggested that you should always dress like you were going to see Mr. or Ms. Right today.

How about your spiritual development? Marriage at its best is not two halves seeking to become a whole but two whole persons who are willing to blend their wholeness into a new unity. Have you discovered the foundation of faith through Christ upon which to build your life? Are you developing personally in your relationship to God? Are you involved in the work of God's kingdom?

How about intellectually? Have you tried to develop your mind? Most people are attracted to interesting individuals who have a wealth of knowledge and who are relatively informed about life.

What is your development socially? Do you use approved table manners or do you look like an animal at feeding time at the zoo? Are you polite and courteous? Do you display the social graces?

How about vocationally? Are you developing your skills and training yourself for a vocation that will fulfill you as a person and enable you to provide for or share the support for a family?

I've known people who married out of desperation because they felt it was their last chance. In some cases it was their only chance. One older single stood up at a testimony meeting to share her favorite verse: "If any man would come after me, let him."

However, if you will develop yourself spiritually, socially, intellectually, physically, and vocationally, you will have a bait that will be attractive to others. Then you won't have to marry out of desperation but can marry through deliberation.

A good model is Jesus whom Luke described in his classic statement: "And Jesus increased in wisdom and in stature, and in favor with God and man" (Luke 2:52, RSV).

FIND THE RIGHT MATE

The next step is to find the right mate. I do not mean the one person on all the earth that God made just for you. I believe there are any number of people with whom you can develop a rewarding marriage. By "the right mate," I mean one with whom you can experience an emotional and psychological compatibility.

This is the key insight of the experience of Isaac. Abraham called his servant and instructed him to find Isaac a mate from his country and his kindred (Gen. 24:4). What did he mean? Abraham knew that Isaac's chances for success in marriage would be enhanced if he married someone from the same social and spiritual background. The commonalities of their lives would provide more likelihood of emotional and psychological compatibility.

The right mate is *one with whom you have some common interests socially*. Happy marriages which combine individuals from dramatically different social or economic backgrounds are usually found only in fairy tales. In real life sociological studies reveal over and over that a common social background makes for the most stable marriage.

In addition, the right mate is *one who possesses emotional maturity*. In a list of qualities unacceptable in a marriage partner, one family expert includes the following: inability to make independent decisions, self-centeredness, lack of self-control, and absence of moral standards.[5] All of these are evidences of an emotional instability which will make a person a poor marriage risk.

Herbert J. Miles draws the comparison between "beautiful Betty" and "balanced Betty." Primary candidates for marriage are usually those whose molecules are so arranged that they are physically attractive. They may have empty heads and cold hearts. But on the outside they are knockouts. Miles suggests that those who dare to look beneath the surface will discover that "balanced Betty," with a well-rounded personality and an emotional stability, is the more promising candidate for a happy marriage mate.[6]

The right mate is also *one with whom you can be spiritually compatible.* A common spiritual foundation is essential to a healthy marriage. Statistics reveal that marriages between people of different religious faiths are fraught with additional pressures. Albert I. Gordon, in his book on intermarriage, concluded, "The statistical evidence, incorporated in this study makes it clear that the 'odds' do not favor intermarriages, in that almost two to four times as many intermarriages as intramarriages end in divorce, separation or annulment."[7]

When we talk about the "right mate," we need to be careful. A person can set such high standards that no one is able to meet them. This will either cause one to miss the good marriage candidates that are available, or it will lead to frustration. Both results are expressed in this touching poem by an unknown, single young lady.

> At sweet sixteen, I first began
> To ask the good Lord for a man;
> At seventeen I recall,
> I wanted someone strong and tall.
> The Christmas I reached eighteen
> I fancied someone blond and lean.
> And then at nineteen, I was sure,
> I'd fall for someone more mature.
> At twenty, I thought I'd find

> Romance with someone with a mind.
> I retrogressed at twenty-one
> And found college boys most fun.
> My viewpoint changed at twenty-two,
> When one man only was my cue.
> I broke my heart at twenty-three,
> And asked for someone kind to me.
> Then begged at blasé twenty-four
> For anyone who wouldn't bore;
> Now, Lord, that I am twenty-five,
> Just send me someone who's alive!

Marriage is too important to enter into with just anyone who is alive. The selective single is one who lets his head be his guide, as well as his heart. For this will lead him to the right mate.

WAIT UNTIL THE RIGHT DATE

There is one more important step, and that is to wait until the right date. Even if you have the right person, your marriage might fail if you get married at the wrong time.

The right time is after an engagement period of several months, during which time the couple tests the degree of satisfaction derived from being exclusively devoted to each other. During this time expectations about marriage should be communicated to each other.

The right time is when, through counseling or study, the individuals are sensitive to the peculiar problems with which marriage will confront them.

The right time is when the couple is financially stable enough to make it on their own. An engaged couple was involved in a marriage course at Pensacola Junior College in Florida. One of the classroom exercises was to project the costs of the first month of married life. After doing the exercise, they decided to postpone their wedding until their pocketbooks could handle the expense.[8]

This can be carried to an extreme as the following poem illustrates.

> The bride bent with age, leaned over her cane,
> Her steps uncertain need guiding,
> While down the church aisle,
>   with a wan toothless smile,
> The groom in a wheel-chair came gliding.
> And who is this elderly couple thus wed?
> You'll find when you've closely explored it,
> That this is that rare, conservative pair . . .
> Who waited TIL THEY COULD AFFORD IT![9]

The basic truth is nevertheless valid. Marriage is not something to jump into capriciously. Enough time needs to elapse during the engagement period to allow you to lay a firm foundation for the future.

CONCLUSION

Many "nice girls" and "great guys" are still single, not because they are indifferent about marriage but because they evaluate marriage so highly. It is serious business to be married. So they are choosy. When they walk down the aisles and commit their lives to other persons, they want it to be at the right rate, with the right mate, at the right date. May the Lord increase their tribe!

4
The Swinging Single: *Dinah*
Genesis 34

What do Coretta King, Elton Trueblood, and Alexander Solzhenitsyn have in common? They all agree on the nature of our problem in America today. In June of 1978, Alexander Solzhenitsyn was the keynote speaker at the graduation ceremonies for Harvard University. In that same month both Coretta King and Elton Trueblood addressed the annual meeting of the Southern Baptist Convention. They similarly concluded that the economic, political, and social dilemmas of our day are merely smoke screens behind which the root cause of our problems is often hidden. Penetrating these smoke screens, each of the three agreed that the real crisis in our day is a crisis in morality.

That the moral crisis is not merely a modern-day matter becomes evident as we consider the story of intrigue and revenge surrounding a single of yesteryear named Dinah.

When Dinah left home to see the world, she became sexually involved with a man named Shechem. Dinah, "a beautiful rebel who had matured physically beyond her years"[1] was sexually abused by Shechem. When her brothers heard what had happened, they were outraged. Carefully, they mapped out a plan for revenge. They agreed to allow Shechem to marry Dinah if all his family would submit to circumcision, but it was simply a ploy. Three days after the men had been circumcised, when they were still physically incapacitated, Dinah's brothers attacked and killed them.

This story of promiscuity, hatred, and revenge stands in contrast to the holiness to which God's children have been called. Nevertheless, it provides some keen insight into the ultimate effect of immorality.

REASONS

The context of the story and the character of the story's primary figure is found in Genesis 34:1. The biblical writer tells us that "Dinah . . . went out to visit the daughters of the land." A couple of questions evolve from that statement.

Who were the daughters of the land? They were the pagan people who inhabited the land. Dinah was not a part of these pagan people. On the contrary, she was a descendant of Abraham to whom God had made some special promises. Abraham and his ancestors were God's chosen people. They were to be holy, and they were to walk in obedience to God. To remain at home would have enabled Dinah to participate in the blessings God had promised to his people and would have maintained her holiness. Rather than being content to remain at home, however, Dinah desired to go out into the world to discover what mysterious pleasures were available there. She opted to become a part of the daughters of the land rather than to remain as a part of the people of God.

A second question is why Dinah would go out. *The Amplified Bible* explains that she went out "unattended." Dangers lurked behind every bush and around every turn for a woman who wandered alone in the land. Safety was assured only in the security of the family abode. Therefore, Dinah was asking for it when she went out to visit the daughters of the land. What motivation compelled Dinah to take such a risk?

Most commentators suggest that restlessness was the motive. Dinah perhaps had become bored with the simple, nomadic life of her father. Life was dull, empty. She wanted excitement. The thrill of the outside world appealed to her. Dinah wanted to go where the people were, to meet the beautiful women, and to mingle with the wide assortment of young men whom she thought were waiting for her out in the world. Like the young man Jesus described in Luke 15, Dinah wanted to see what life was like in the city. Boredom demanding stimulation, emptiness craving fulfillment—those were the motives that drove her out of her father's house. She was lured by the scintillating promises of the world which she felt would provide meaning in her life.

Emptiness and a quest for meaning are a part of the fabric of life as we know it today. The promise of excitement is a strong stimulant. Strangely, it is not the preachers but the psychologists who are heralding this meaninglessness in the life of modern man.

Carl Jung, the famous Swiss psychiatrist, said that "the central neurosis of our time is emptiness." Rollo May, a New York psychologist agreed. "On the basis of my clinical practice as well as that of my psychological and psychiatric colleagues," May stated, "the chief problem of people in the middle . . . of the twentieth century is emptiness." Victor Frankl sounded the same note when he said, "The state of inner-emptiness is at present one of the major challenges to psychiatry."[2]

Where is the answer to the meaninglessness of life to be found? Many seek fulfillment in a life of promiscuity. They, like Dinah, go out to visit the daughters of the land. Sexual adventure seems to offer an escape from the dull sameness of their lives.

A young single shared with me how this happened to her. Her life had been sheltered in the small town where she grew up. Life was so boring that a person could gather a crowd by simply clearing his throat! What a change when she came to Dallas. The glittering lights, the ever-present temptations, the compulsion of the crowd, and the exciting stimulation of the city coaxed her into a life of sexual permissiveness. She did things she had never thought she would. She became a swinging single. Why? Because she felt that permissiveness was the pathway which would fill the void in her life.

In such a case as this permissiveness is not the problem but a sign of an even deeper problem which is an inner emptiness. Permissiveness becomes the tool by which a person seeks to assert his value and worth as an individual.

Why did Dinah leave home? One explanation is that she was motivated by restlessness and a desire for excitement. Another possible explanation is that she was motivated by the restrictions of her home and a desire for freedom. Dinah had perhaps become tired of the restrictions placed on her by her father. She may have thought there were too many rules. Even though some commentators think Jacob allowed her a great deal of freedom, she wanted to be freer. She wanted to get away from home so that she could do all the things that she had fantasized and dreamed about.

This, too, often happens today. A young person goes to college or gets an apartment of his own. A single leaves the town where he grew up and suddenly experiences the anonymity which the city provides. Now he is free. The parents are no longer there to demand a certain kind of behavior. Gone are the scrutinizing eyes of the town gossips. The control of community mores is removed. He is free. Joining with the permissive crowd then becomes a way to assert this newly gained freedom.

If there is anything which is praised and desired today, it is freedom, freedom to experiment and experience, freedom to do what we want to do. When Mick Jagger of the Rolling Stones was arrested for illegal possession of drugs, he asserted, "It's when authority won't allow something that I dig in. I'm against anything that interferes with individual freedom."[3] That philosophy motivates many today. Inhibited by the laws of God and deprived because of the disciplines of morality, many individuals adopt lifestyles of permissiveness to enjoy and express their freedom.

Do you know that God wants you to be free? God's Son announced that he had come "to proclaim release to the captives . . . to set free those who are downtrodden" (Luke 4:18). Freedom is good. Freedom is to be desired. Freedom to become all that you were made to be is the predominant chord of the gospel message. God wants you to be free!

Why then do so many turn from God's way to find the freedom they desire? And why do so many find in permissiveness not freedom but bondage of the worse sort? Two factors are at the foundation of this paradox.

Confusion about where freedom is to be found is part of the problem. God does not enslave man. Sin does. Since God made us, he knows what will make us free. Because God loves us, he has given us the road signs which will lead us to that freedom. These road signs are found in his Word. Disobedience to God's Word does not bring freedom. Instead, it deprives us of freedom.

"When lust has conceived, it gives birth to sin; and when sin is accomplished, it brings forth death" (Jas. 1:15). That's the ultimate outcome of permissiveness. Spell it b-o-n-d-a-g-e.

"If you abide in My word, then you are truly disciples of Mine; and you shall know the truth, and the truth shall make you free" (John 8:31-32). That's the ultimate outcome of living life God's way. Spell it f-r-e-e-d-o-m.

Another part of the confusion concerns the meaning of freedom. Freedom is not the right to do as you please. No one has that kind of freedom. Freedom is the ability to do as you ought. It is freedom from sin, freedom from the pressure of the crowd, freedom from the motivation of the moment, freedom from the fear of tomorrow, freedom from the smallness of self, freedom to be all that God made you to be—that's freedom. That kind of freedom is not found by "visiting the daughters of the land" but by living in fellowship with the Father.

Dinah left home to visit the daughters of the land. Whether it was a search for excitement or a desire for freedom that motivated her, Dinah became involved in a sexual relationship that threatened the welfare of her entire family and distorted her own sense of values. The Bible says Shechem "saw her, he took her and lay with her by force" (Gen. 34:2). With staccato swiftness, Shechem abused and misused Dinah. Yet, as the story unfolds, she evidently was willing to marry him. Her pride had vanished. Her sense of right and wrong had lost its power of discernment. Her promenade into permissiveness did not lead to life but to death, not to fulfillment but to a deeper emptiness.

RESTRICTIONS

Despite such obvious lessons, many singles today are nevertheless hot on Dinah's trail. Driven by a desire for excitement and freedom, many singles become swingers (or "swingles"). Permissiveness becomes their watchword. How can such a pattern be avoided? Four deterrents often block the pathway that leads to permissiveness.

Conscience is one of the deterrents. The dictionary defines conscience as "the faculty by which distinctions are made between moral right and wrong, especially in regard to one's own conduct."[4] And everybody has one. It might not be of the Jiminy Crickett variety a la Pinocchio. But everybody has one. Gail Sheehy calls it our "inner custodian."[5] Many are blocked from the road to permissiveness by an active conscience which says: Don't. It's not right.

A couple of problems exist in relationship with the conscience. One problem is that everyone's conscience is not shaped by the same forces. We all have a sense of oughtness, but the content of that oughtness differs from individual to individual. This was illustrated by Hitler who exterminated Jews without any twinge of conscience, and Susan Atkins of the Manson family who evaluated her involvement in the murder of seven people by saying, "I knew it was right because it felt good."

Another problem is that the conscience can be ignored. As one little boy put it, "We all have a spark of conscience. But sometimes we don't clean the spark plugs often enough!" Our conscience points out the roads that are available. It does not always determine which road we take.

Another deterrent is *custom*. This is the outward custodian. Each community has its customary way of doing things, its mores. *Mores* are defined as "the established, traditional customs or folkways regarded by a social group as essential to its preservation and welfare."[6]

It is obvious that the force of this deterrent has been lessened in the last couple of decades by the rapid degree of change in society. In addition, the automobile makes it possible to quickly escape from the confines of custom. And the mobility in American society has placed customs on a somewhat unsure footing. Statistics indicate that about one-fifth of the total American population moves each year. When the 1970 census was taken, 47 percent of the people had been at their present address fewer than five years. All of these factors have contributed to a lessening power of custom in determining moral behavior.

Circumstances can also be a deterrent to permissiveness.

Morality is often only a matter of insufficient opportunities. The problem with this deterrent is that circumstances can change. Opportunities for immorality will come. If circumstances alone are the deterrent, eventually an individual will practice permissiveness when the opportunities arise.

A fourth deterrent to permissiveness is *commitment*. Commitment finds its foundation not in what we think is right but what the Bible says. It is not shaped by custom; it shapes custom. It is not determined by circumstances; it is constant in all circumstances. It is the kind of commitment expressed by young Jonathan Edwards several centuries ago. As a nineteen-year-old man, he recorded this resolution in his diary: "Resolved: That every man should live to the glory of God. Resolved Second: That whether others do this or not, I will.'" That's commitment!

Dinah turned off her conscience and sought to escape from the confines of custom. Circumstances were not favorable at home for her desires to be filled, so she went out to visit the daughters of the land. She lacked the commitment that would have curbed permissiveness.

REMEDY

Of the deterrents to permissiveness, commitment is the key. The conscience can be programmed to conform to the crowd. Circumstances constantly change. The power of custom is often diluted by the anonymity of the city or escaped by the mobility of the automobile. Only commitment can be a constant companion in every circumstance. Inner commitment which determines outward behavior is the remedy for permissiveness.

What does commitment mean? It means to desire to do God's will and follow God's way in every relationship and in all situations. Commitment's theme song is not "I Did

It My Way" but "I Did It God's Way."

But how is God's way to be discerned? In 1 Corinthians 6, Paul provided some principles which will help. One suggestion Paul made was the *holiness principle*. "Do you not know that the unrighteous shall not inherit the kingdom of God?" (1 Cor. 6:9). Then, he specifically stated what he meant by unrighteousness. Paul did not mean that if you do the things listed then you are not a Christian and can never be one. Rather, he reminded us that we have been redeemed from these things, set apart from them. This is a basic premise of the Scriptures. Some things are to be excluded from the life of the Christian, single or married, because Jesus "gave Himself for us, that He might redeem us from every lawless deed and purify for Himself a people for His own possession" (Titus 2:14).

Where are these things found that are to be excluded from the life of the Christian? In God's Word. Some specific places to start are Exodus 20; Proverbs 6:16-19; Matthew 5—7; Romans 1:28-32; Galatians 5:19-21; and 1 Corinthians 6:9-11.

Because of the life of holiness to which we have been called as Christians, some things are wrong for us because God has said so in his Word.

Then Paul suggested the *help principle*. Some things which are not specifically restricted in God's Word are nevertheless to be avoided by the Christian because of what Paul suggested in 1 Corinthians 6:12: "All things are lawful for me, but not all things are profitable." They do not build the individual up. They do not develop the person toward spiritual maturity. Therefore, they are to be avoided.

O. Hobart Mowrer has correctly concluded, "The folly of eat, drink and be merry for tomorrow we die, is that we usually don't die tomorrow but live to reap the consequences of short sighted pleasure.''[8]

That there are consequences for every action is a fact written into the moral framework of the universe. It is inevitable. Thus, the Christian must carefully analyze the ultimate result of his action.

Let me illustrate how this principle works. I know of no place in God's Word that says, "Thou shalt not peruse a *Playboy* magazine or go to an X-rated movie." These things are not unlawful. However, when a Christian single realizes that such actions can confuse his understanding of human sexuality, create unhealthy desires, and clutter the mind with filth, he will probably conclude that such activities are to be avoided.

Our challenge is to do those things which build us up physically, morally, mentally, and spiritually. When you face a moral decision for which you have no specific statement in the Scriptures, commitment will lead you to ask: Does it build? Is it good for me in the long run?

A third suggestion is the *habit principle*. In the same twelfth verse, Paul said, "All things are lawful for me, but I will not be mastered by anything." It may be translated: "I may do as I please with anything but I will not let anything do as it pleases with me" (author).

G. Campbell Morgan, the outstanding English expositor, one day faced the issue of his pipe. He took the clay pipe of which he was so fond and said, "You are becoming my master instead of my servant." Snapping it in pieces, he tossed it into the fire.[9] The power of habit is not to take precedence over the power of God.

Our challenge is to follow the will of God. When you face a moral decision with no specific statement in the Scriptures, commitment will lead you to ask: Is this habit-forming? Will this action set a precedent in my life?

Paul suggested a fourth aid to morality, the *honor prin-*

ciple. "For you have been bought with a price: therefore glorify God in your body" (1 Cor. 6:20). To "glorify God" means to make him look good to the world, to project a favorable image of God to the world. It means to honor him.

The Bible clearly states that in everything he does, the Christian is to glorify God (Matt. 5:16). In simple language that means whenever you are faced by a moral decision and have no direct declaration in the Scriptures, commitment will lead you to ask: Does this action make God look good? Does it enhance God's reputation in the world?

When Dinah went out to visit the daughters of the land, she did what God had specifically prohibited. Her newly established relationship was not helpful to her or to her family. It certainly did not glorify either God or his people. Jacob's anguished cry to his sons accurately describes the ultimate result of Dinah's adventure: "You have brought trouble on me by making me odious among the inhabitants of the land" (Gen. 34:30).

The remedy for permissiveness is commitment to the principles that lead to holiness. Will it be easy? No. Commitment to God's way is never easy. But it will provide a sense of meaning that can be discovered nowhere else. In addition, such commitment will free an individual to become all that God made him to be.

CONCLUSION

Remember when Moses came down from Mount Sinai to the waiting Hebrews (Ex. 32). He carried the tablets upon which were etched the laws of God. These were the stipulations by which their relationship with God was to be determined. The "anti-adultery clause" stayed in, as did all the other Commandments.

The anti-adultery clause does stay in. Permissiveness and Christian discipleship do not mix. A Christian is to live in the context of God's purpose rather than dwelling among the daughters of the land. Had Dinah only realized that, her entire life might have been different.

5
The Singing Single: *Miriam*
Exodus 2:4, 15:20-21; Numbers 26:59

In the days long before women's lib, the Germans limited the realm of womanhood to the four K's: *kinder* (children), *kleiden* (clothing), *kuche* (kitchen), and *kirche* (church).[1] To be prepared for her role, a women needed to be taught only enough geography to know how to get from one room to another in the house and the only chemistry she needed was how to follow a recipe.[2] Throughout the centuries, such has usually been the role relegated to women.

Not all women, however, have been willing to fit within that narrow niche which society had carved out for them. Instead, they rose above the crowd to make a significant contribution to society. A prime example was Miriam, sister of Moses and a leader of the Hebrews. For our purposes, it needs to be pointed out that Miriam was not only a woman but more than likely a single as well.

One tradition asserts that Miriam was married to Hur, the one who, along with Aaron, held up the hands of Moses in one of the battles of the Hebrews (Ex. 17:12). However, there is no hint of such a marriage in the Scriptures. The clear implication of the Bible is that Miriam never married. She was another of the singles of the Bible.

Our first glimpse of Miriam reveals the courage and keenness of mind that so characterized her life (Ex. 2). An edict had been given to kill all the male Hebrew children. To protect him, Moses' mother put him in a basket in the water and left Miriam to watch over him. Pharaoh's daughter discovered the baby while she was taking a bath. For some reason, which is never explained, she decided to keep the baby for her own.

Miriam witnessed the discovery of Moses and saw, with great excitement, what Pharaoh's daughter decided to do. With undaunted courage, Miriam approached the daughter of Pharaoh and told her she would find someone to nurse the baby. Pharaoh's daughter agreed, and immediately Miriam went to get her mother. By this unusual twist of circumstances, Moses' own mother had the privilege of caring for her son while he was very young, and he had the privilege of being raised in the household of Pharaoh.

Later portraits of Miriam build on and expand these initial reflections of courage and keenness of mind. Let's look at her life and see what we can learn.

THE GOOD NEWS

Miriam was no minor character in the unfolding drama of Hebrew history. On the contrary, she was a key figure whose story is woven together inextricably with the story of her two brothers, Moses and Aaron. Moses was selected by God as the leader of the Hebrew people and as their deliverer from Egyptian bondage. Aaron was appointed by God as the spokesman for Moses. Miriam's prominence was not something that grew out of her divine appointment, but rather it developed from her strong and courageous spirit.

Several aspects of her achievement and character are clearly described in the Scriptures. This is the good news about her.

The Bible pictures her as a *patriot*. Eugenia Price calls her "the first woman patriot mentioned in the Bible."[3] Exodus 15:20-21 seems to show Miriam in a position of responsibility over the Hebrew women. This was a critical time in Hebrew history. The Hebrews were just beginning to emerge as a distinct people. They had been delivered from Egyptian slavery. Under the direction of Moses, the Hebrews were ready to move toward the land that had been promised to them. No one person, however, could bring about the fulfillment of their hopes. Total commitment of the people was required. Miriam willingly filled her place of responsibility as a patriot.

At the close of the Constitutional Convention in 1787, Benjamin Franklin is reported to have said, "We have given you a republic—if you can keep it."[4] That is the challenge of every generation.

In no generation has the challenge been greater than in our day. Who has not been outraged by the proliferation of pornography in our land? Who is not troubled about the pressures and problems our homes are facing? Who is not disturbed at the general collapse of morals in our land? Who is not dismayed by the increasing emphasis on materialism? Who is not appalled at the corruption that continues to be uncovered at every level of state and national government? The question that the psalmist raised long ago is appropriate for our day: "If the foundations are destroyed, /What can the righteous do?" (Ps. 11:3).

The answer is the same today as it was in Miriam's day. The righteous must be willing to commit themselves to God. What does that mean? It means simply that we must cultivate those things that really count.

So often we get our priorities confused. Some figures I saw recently startled me. In one year (1975), we Americans spent 2 billion dollars on movies. In the same year we spent 250 million dollars on mouthwash. In Egg Harbor, New Jersey, there is a retirement home for elderly dogs with yellow-tiled bathing facilities where people pay up to 140 dollars a month to have their retired dogs taken care of.

I like to go to the movie every once in awhile, I like dogs, and I'm all for mouthwash. But somewhere along the line we are going to have to decide which things are really important in life and commit ourselves, our resources, and our finances to cultivating those things. Integrity is important and must be cultivated. Our religious institutions are important and must be supported. Our structure of democratic government is important and must be maintained.

"If the foundations are destroyed,/What can the righteous do?" We can commit ourselves to cultivating those things that really count. We often hear the statement of Carl Schurz, "Our country right or wrong." But that was not all of the statement. This is what he said: "Our country right or wrong. When right to keep it right. When wrong to put it right." That ought to be the commitment of every Christian citizen.

These are crucial days in our nation. As Miriam did in her generation, so must our committed singles of today willingly fill their places of responsibility as patriots.

Miriam was also called a *prophetess* (Ex. 15:20). The word connotes one who was inspired and directed to teach the will of God. She was not only involved in leading the people but also was involved in worshiping God. This subject will be discussed further in chapter 8. Suffice it to say here that there is a growing awareness in the church that the qualification for being a teacher is not your marital status but whether you have been inspired and directed to teach the will of God. Doors are opening for singles in the church.

Miriam was also what I would call a *positivist*. The Bible says that after successfully crossing the Red Sea, Miriam called out the women to sing unto the Lord a song of victory (Ex. 15:21). There was nothing negative about her personality. She had a positive attitude that permeated everything she did.

Such positivism was unusual among the Hebrews of her day, as the grumbling of the people detailed in Exodus 16 indicates. Such positivism is equally unusual today. Ours is a critical age, a day of pessimism. Someone is always ready to lead in a word of criticism. One guy was called "Whiplash" because he was such a pain in the neck. Many singles fall into the habit of singing their single blues. We are refreshed when we find someone who looks for the best rather than the worst, who encourages rather than criticizes. Miriam was such a person.

Pessimism is a blight which causes several problems in our lives and in society. For one thing, pessimism cramps our creativity. The problem with pessimism is not that it is not justified. Many times it is. The problem is that it produces lethargy. It keeps us from trying because we are convinced in the beginning that something cannot be done. The things in life that have been accomplished have been done by those unwilling to accept that they couldn't be done. While others stand around saying, "It can't be done," they have already done it. Pessimism blocks the door to that kind of creative accomplishment.

Pessimism also perpetuates our past. A pessimist is one who looks at the past failures of his life and knows that he can expect only more of the same in the future. It is a painful prison from which he cannot break free. The optimist sees the past, even with its failures, as building blocks for a more important future.

In addition, pessimism frustrates our future. Pessimism casts a dark shadow of impossibility over our future. But think of what optimism does. I heard of one ninety-five-year-old man who bought a suit and got two pairs of pants with it. He got married and bought a house next to an elementary school! There was a man who was making plans for the future.

If Miriam would have carefully analyzed the situation in which the Hebrews found themselves, perhaps she could have become pessimistic. Instead, with a positive spirit of optimism, she thanked God for what he had done in the past and trusted him with what he could do in the future. She was a positivist!

What does it take for a single woman to be successful? Marilyn McGinnis in her book on singles suggests three steps: look like a woman, act like a lady, and think like a man.[5]

Miriam offers another option. Her success came because of the positive spirit with which she became involved in both worship and leadership. That was the good news about her.

THE BAD NEWS

There was another side to Miriam, however, as Numbers 12 reveals. A dark cloud fell across the life of this impressive single, for the Bible says, "Miriam and Aaron spoke against Moses" (Num. 12:1). Moses was God's appointed leader. Instead of acknowledging his leadership, Miriam sought to undermine it. In doing so, she was not just opposing her brother. She was setting herself in opposition to God. This positivist, who had been both prophetess and patriot, now experienced the reality of disobedience. Her story of success was spoiled by sin.

Why did Miriam turn on Moses? The biblical writer attributed her rebellion to Moses' choice of an Ethiopian to be his wife (Num. 12:1). Perhaps she spoke out against Moses because she was jealous of him. This is the implication of Numbers 12:2. Eugenia Price suggests that Miriam was jealous for Moses' time. That is, a new wife would divert his attention further from the task at hand.

Miriam had dedicated herself completely to the cause. Why could not Moses do as much?[6]

Discovering the reason for Miriam's sin is not as important as recognizing the fact of her sin. This gifted single of yesteryear, who had so much going for her, now faced the fact of failure. Sin invaded her life. If she experienced the reality of sin, so can we today. Not one of us is immune to sin. No one goes through life completely sidestepping failure. We need to accept that fact about ourselves. Paul gave this testimony in Romans 3:12: "All have turned away from God;/they have all gone wrong;/no one does what is right, not even one" (TEV).

When you, like Miriam, allow sin to come into your life, what can you do about it: Several steps will lead you out of the darkness back into the light.

First, *refuse to let your sin defeat you.* The tragedy of most lives is not that we sin but that we allow our sin to defeat us. When sin has knocked you off your feet, don't stay there. Get back up.

When the Hebrew children entered the Promised Land under the leadership of Joshua, they won a magnificent victory at Jericho. However, one of the Hebrews disobeyed God. Sin entered their ranks. The result was an ignominious defeat at Ai. Shattered by their defeat, "the hearts of the people melted, and became as water" (Josh. 7:5, RSV). Joshua, their leader, "rent his clothes, and fell to the earth upon his face before the ark of the Lord" (v. 6, RSV). They were defeated by their sin.

Do you know what God told Joshua and the Hebrews? "Arise," he said, "sanctify the people" (Josh. 7:10,13, RSV). "Get back on your feet, and move forward again" (author's paraphrase). That is what God told them. Do not let your sin defeat you. Rise up and sanctify yourself.

But how? That's the second step: *repent of that sin.* The mark of the real Christian is not that he never sins but that he does not dwell in his sin. He does not continue in the habit of sin. Instead, the moment he realizes what he has done, he wants to turn away from it. One pastor put it like this: "The pagan leaps into sin and loves it. The Christian lapses into sin and loathes it!" There is a difference in the way we react to sin.

When you realize that sin has slipped into your life, confess that sin to God. There is no other way that sin can be taken care of. You cannot cover it up. You cannot excuse it away. You cannot escape responsibility for it. You cannot talk your way out of it. You have to confess it. And this is the promise of God's Word: "If we confess our sins, He is faithful and righteous to forgive us our sins and to cleanse us from all unrighteousness" (1 John 1:9).

The third step is to *release the sin.* The problem with so many of us is that after we have confessed our sin, we hold on to it. We carry it around as a burden. We allow it to continually darken our lives. We hold on to it. We need to remember that God has forgiven our sin, and so can we.

The fourth step is to *refocus our lives.* The writer of Hebrews gives a beautiful admonition for all of us. "Therefore, since we have so great a cloud of witnesses surrounding us, let us also lay aside every encumbrance, and the sin which so easily entangles us, and let us run with endurance the race that is set before us, fixing our eyes on Jesus, the author and perfecter of faith" (Heb. 12:1-2).

Phillips Brooks, one of the greatest pulpiteers in American history, was single. From 1860-1891 he was the spiritual leader of Trinity Church in Boston, where he literally transformed that city for Christ. Other than the unique endowment of talent that God gave him, the secret of his life was something his mother had told him. Time and time again she had repeated to her son, "Philly, keep close to Christ."

An intense focus on Christ and an intimate walk with Christ is the best antidote to temptation. Had Miriam kept her eyes on God, instead of putting them on Moses, perhaps she would have avoided this serious blight on her life.

CONCLUSION

This singing single of the past was indeed a success. Hers is one of the inspiring pictures of the contribution of a single to God's work. Her success came not because she was immune to failure and above sin but because she refused to let her failure and sin deter her. God used her despite her sin.

6
The Sorrowful Single: *Naomi*

Ruth

It was one of those visits that was both stimulating and sad, stimulating because of the strong faith of the woman nearly eighty-two years old who had been a member of our church for years, sad because her husband was no longer with her to share that faith. She was a widow.

As we visited, my eyes surveyed the room which was filled with pictures and other memorabilia from her life with her husband. Although her spirit was optimistic and self-pity was altogether absent, there was nevertheless an underlying sorrow in her life. Without her husband there was an incompleteness about her life that she had never been able to overcome. Death had taken from her a part of her life. She had never really recovered.

A widow of yesteryear experienced that same sense of loss and the same degree of sorrow. Her name was Naomi, and her story is told in the book of Ruth.

Naomi and her husband Elimelech left Judah because of a famine. Moving with their two sons, they set up their residence in Moab. When the sons grew up they married local girls. Unexpectedly, the three men died. The loss of her two sons and her husband was traumatic for Naomi. Bitter at the way life had treated her, she decided to return home to pick up the pieces. Her bitterness was reflected in her desire to change her name from Naomi to Mara which means "bitter," a symbol of the bitter way which she felt God had treated her (Ruth 1:20).

Ruth, one of the daughters-in-law, went back to Judah

with her. The story of Ruth's quest for Boaz and their eventual marriage is one of the Bible's most beautiful love stories. The event around which Ruth's life revolved was her new husband.[1]

The event around which Naomi's life revolved was the loss of her husband and her adjustment to the life of widowhood. We can learn some lessons on coping with death from her experience.

THE INEVITABILITY OF DEATH

When Naomi was married, she fully expected to live with her husband well into old age. Life is so full of excitement and vitality that death, when it is considered at all, is seen as nothing more than a remote possibility. It is something that happens to "old people" or to others. We don't think about the possibility of death for us and our loved ones. Someday we must all face the fact, as Naomi eventually did, that death is an inevitable part of our lives.

The Bible confirms this conclusion. The writer of Hebrews suggested, "It is appointed for men to die once and after this comes judgment" (9:27). The writer of Ecclesiastes reminded us that there was "a time to give birth, and a time to die" (3:2). The psalmist asked rhetorically, "What man can live and not see death?" (89:48).

From the time God said to man in the Garden of Eden, "If you eat of the fruit of the tree you shall surely die" (Gen. 2:17, author's paraphrase) death has been an inevitable part of the experience of every man. Death will come eventually to you and to your mate. To accept that fact is to take the first step in facing it when it happens.

A conspiracy of silence, however, is at work trying to deny the fact of death. Geoffrey Gorer, an English sociologist, concluded that in contemporary culture the personal event of death has replaced sex as the taboo subject.

Death talk has replaced sex talk as the unmentionable.[2]

Part of this silence is understandable. Like the Jews who, out of respect for the awesomeness of God, would not pronounce the name of Yahweh, so we, out of respect for the awesomeness of death, often find it difficult to bring the word *death* to our lips.[3] Reticence for that reason is understandable. On the other hand, when we like King Louis XV of France forbid the word *death* from being mentioned in our presence because we do not want to face up to our mortality, then we are living in a dream world. One counselee told me that she and her husband did not have a will because "he didn't want to think about needing one." He is due for a rude awakening one of these days. Death is a reality of life. All of our silence cannot change that fact.

When we do speak of death, we often try to further soften its reality by use of euphemisms. A euphemism is a word or phrase used to describe something which is less direct, less expressive, or less offensive. Thus we say about a dead person that he "has passed" or "has left" us or "has gone to be with the Lord" or "has expired" or is "really only asleep." Seldom do we simply say, "He is dead."

Neither our silence nor our euphemisms, however, can deny the fact that what happened to Naomi's husband will someday happen to each of us. It will happen to your mate as well.

I like the way one man from Arizona put it. When asked what the death rate was in Arizona, he said, "Same as it is where you live—one to a person."

The narrative of Naomi's life shows that she and her husband walked side by side for a number of years. Then he was gone. Death had taken him and left her a widow. His demise reminds us that death is an inevitable experience in every life.

THE IMPACT OF DEATH

Not only did Naomi have to face the inevitability of death but she also had to face the impact of death on her own life. Paul Harvey, the news commentator, concluded that the loss of a spouse is the number one stress experience in life. Vance Havner said, after the loss of his beloved Sara, "One thing is certain, when your dearest leaves you for heaven and you plod on alone—there can be no harder blow, no greater human bereavement."[4]

The evidence of this stress is seen in Naomi's life. The Bible says that she "was bereft of her two children and her husband" (Ruth 1:5). "Have I yet sons in my womb," she cried, "that they may be your husbands?" (Ruth 1:11). "It is harder for me than for you," she added, "for the hand of the Lord has gone forth against me" (Ruth 1:13). The clearest expression of her grief was this, "Do not call me Naomi; call me Mara, for the Almighty has dealt very bitterly with me. I went out full, but the Lord has brought me back empty. Why do you call me Naomi, since the Lord has witnessed against me and the Almighty has afflicted me?" (Ruth 1:20-21).

Naomi was in a bad condition. The entire story is punctuated with the pulsations of passion. What an impact the death of a spouse makes on our lives!

After the death of his beloved wife, C. S. Lewis said that the pain was not localized in certain places, at certain times, or on certain days as he thought it would be. Instead, he discovered that it made every part of every day different. Her absence, Lewis stated, was like the sky, spread over everything.[5]

Death hurts! That's what C. S. Lewis said. That's what Naomi experienced. Sometimes the degree of hurt is not immediately discernible. The sudden shock makes the surviving mate seem stronger than he or she is. One widow explained this phenomenon by saying, "On the surface I seemed only bruised; on the inside my heart was broken."

As the shock wears off, the depth of the disruption soon becomes evident. Consider some of the elements of this impact.

The death of a mate makes a *personal impact*. Death ushers in a status change which is often accompanied by an identity crisis. "We" language is no longer appropriate. Yet, it was in that "we-ness" that our identity was centered. Now, a new search has to be initiated to determine who we are and what we are to do with our lives.

Naomi faced that crisis. Alone in a strange land, she decided that her self-identity could be regained in the context of familiar people and familiar traditions. Thus, she returned to her homeland.

There is also an *emotional impact*. Nothing so stirs the emotions like the trauma of death. Often the loss of a mate dredges up the emotion of guilt. "If only . . ." is a common grief reaction that I have heard. Regrets at not having met a need, expressed a thought, provided a pleasure—these are a part of the aftermath of grief. We wish that the past could have been better.

At the other end of the spectrum is an emotional idealization of the past. The daily dilemmas of married life forced reality on us. The imperfections of our mate were ever present. This was expressed by the preacher's wife who responded to a church member's exclamation, "Oh, how wonderful your husband is," with a dose of realism, "You ought to live with him!" Living with each other reminds us of our imperfections. When the person is gone, however, the absence of the person causes myths to arise, and no reality is there to check them.

Both of these emotional reactions are to be expected and can be temporarily accepted. There were both negative and positive aspects of our relationship with our mate.

Our attention will be focused on one and then the other in the grief process. The danger of permanently living in the world of "if only" or "it was so wonderful" is that it locks a person into the past. Both emotions focus on the past. Life, however, is to be lived in the present. Today is really all we have. A healthy adjustment to death has been reached when a person is more concerned about the positive possibilities of today than the negative inadequacies of yesterday, when he is more committed to experience a quality life in the present than to enjoy the quality life that he experienced in the past.

Naomi knew this dilemma too. She was an emotional wreck when she returned to her homeland. Eventually, she seems to have redirected her concentration from the past to the present, from concern for the welfare of self to concern for the welfare of Ruth. Read the first chapter and then the third chapter of Ruth. The change in Naomi is dramatic. It reveals a healthy development in her grief process.

A *social impact* also results from the death of a mate. Not only in our own eyes but also in the eyes of society, our status was measured by our "we-ness." Immediately following the loss of our mate, our friends usually give splendid support. Often, however, as time passes, they return to their normal routine of a couple-oriented life in which three is a crowd.

Those dealing with people in the process of dying suggest that one of their greatest fears is that of isolation. Many times, the dying patient will isolate himself. More often, the isolation is caused by his confinement in intensive care units and by the reticence of the family to talk with him about the experience through which he is going.

This fear of isolation, it seems to me, is as much a problem for the one who remains as for the one who is dying. Much of social life and even church life is couple oriented.

For a wife, a large part of her social life was dictated by her relationship with her husband. All of that changes with the experience of death.

No doubt Naomi experienced this isolation in Moab. Even when she returned to Judah it was still there. No longer was she the wife of Elimelech. She was alone. Her social status had changed.

Another part of the aftermath of death is a *spiritual impact.* Inevitably the questions will arise. Why did this happen to me? Why now? Where is God when I need him? Why has God dealt with me so tragically? Why is God silent? Where is God? Is there a God?

I've had many people say, "I don't question God. It's his will." That's admirable. Somewhere in the process of losing a loved one, however, I believe that all of us will at least ask some questions of God.

Naomi's spiritual trauma was apparent. We see evidence of the same thing in the life of Job when his family was taken from him by death. It is significant in both of their experiences to note that in the spiritual dilemma, they turned *to* God with their questions, not *from* God, because they knew that it was in God that the answers would eventually come.

Charles Spurgeon, the British preacher, once said that God is too good to be unkind, too wise to be mistaken, and when you cannot trace his hand, you can always trust his heart.

For the Christian, spiritual stability comes in the promise of one who faced death, won the victory over it, and shares that victory with us. Paul expressed this promise in his words of assurance, "For I am convinced that neither death, nor life, nor angels, nor principalities, nor things present, nor things to come, nor powers, nor height, nor depth, nor any other created thing, shall be able to separate us from the love of God, which is in Christ Jesus our

Lord'' (Rom. 8:38-39). Neither death nor life can separate us from God. That is why, like Spurgeon, even when we cannot trace God's hand, we can most certainly trust his heart.

Make no mistake about it. Death hurts. And the traumatic impact of death affects every aspect of our life.

THE IMPLICATIONS OF DEATH

What then are we to do in the face of death? Every fifteen seconds someone dies in our country. What are the implications of this inevitable experience that so dramatically impacts our life? Let me give some general principles which are applicable to you whether you are the one who lost the mate or whether you are trying to help a widow or widower deal with their loss.

One implication is *the necessity of a process of mourning.* Grief, as one man has defined it, is the experience through which we help our feelings catch up with the fact of what has happened in our life.[6] If not worked out in a healthy way, these emotions will be internalized, resulting in internal conflict or interpersonal difficulties later on.

A beautiful example is Jesus' relationship with Mary and Martha. Lazarus, their brother and Jesus' friend, had died. When Jesus came to them they were in a deep state of grief. Jesus did not reprimand them for it. Rather he felt it with them. He shared it. He let them talk about it. He even cried (John 11).

When someone you love dies, it hurts. Mourning is a natural, healthy way to work through the hurt. We need to encourage it.

Another implication is *the need to support the mourners.* This means to stand by them as a friend, to be there to help. Every widow and widower needs a friend who really cares.

One man has pointed out five symptoms of acute grief

in the life of a mourner which can be danger signs: (1) somatic distress such as sighing, shortness of breath, and fatigue; (2) preoccupation with the image of the deceased; (3) an inordinate guilt; (4) hostility to everyone around them; and (5) loss of common patterns of conduct.[7]

As followers of Christ who have been commanded to "bear one another's burdens" (Gal. 6:2), we should be sensitive enough to the mourners that when these danger signals appear, we can set our lives next to theirs so that we can provide comfort, relief, and strength.

A third vital step is to *reinvolve the mourners in society.* Extreme sensitivity must be shown at this point. The emotional development of the mourner must be understood. Nevertheless, the fact remains that a return to healthy life will involve a reestablishment of relationships and a forging of a new social identity. Sometimes assistance is needed for a widow or widower to do that.

One widow went through a prolonged period of mourning. Internal turmoil and interpersonal trauma with her son marred her life. A serious confrontation with her son finally jarred her to her senses. She concluded that her real problem was not self-pity or hurt but fear of reentering life. She had withdrawn for so long that she was terrified of actually facing life again. She had hidden too long in the shadow, so she acted. She obtained a new job, began to establish some new relationships, and gradually moved into life again. Her son's not-so-gentle nudge was the key.[8]

What that son did for his mother, Ruth did for Naomi. From her preoccupation with death, Naomi began to be interested in life again because of Ruth. That is a necessary step in overcoming the traumatic confrontation with the death of a mate.

Through it all, we must also *remember the answer for death.* Several years ago a family visited Carlsbad Caverns. When the group reached the lowest part of the cave, the guide suddenly flipped off the lights to show how dark it was beneath the surface. The darkness was interrupted by two sounds: the muffled cry of the little girl in the family shocked by the sudden darkness and the reassuring words of her older brother, "Don't worry, Sis. There's someone here who knows how to turn on the lights."

When the sudden darkness of death settles down on our lives, remember that in Christ we have found someone who knows how to turn on the light!

7
The Sterling Single: *Vashti*
Esther 1; 2:1; 4:7

As the couple sat down in the pastor's office, their unhappiness was evident. Only a few years before they had stood before this same pastor with stars in their eyes and a shared dream of what their life could be like together. Now the stars were gone. Gone also were the dreams. Their marriage was on the rocks. The pastor addressed the lady. "Joan," he said, "at your wedding ceremony you promised to take Jim for better or for worse."

"That's right," she responded, "but he is worse than I took him for!"

That tragic discovery confronts many individuals in the marriage game. Before marriage the husband appears to be gallant, generous, and gentle. Once he has walked down the aisle, he becomes grim, gross, and gripey. Before the wedding, the bride seems to be the catch of the century. "How lucky he is to get her," friends say, and the groom agrees. But soon her real identity emerges, and the conversation changes. Says the wife, "You don't deserve a wife like me."

The husband replies, "I don't deserve asthma either, but I've got it." "For better or worse" is drowned out in the realization that his mate is worse than he took her for.

After sixty years of marriage one lady appeared before a judge requesting a divorce from her husband. "After sixty years, why on earth do you want a divorce now?" the judge wanted to know.

"Because, enough is enough!" was her reply.

When does enough become enough? Granted that nobody is perfect, what is the limit of unacceptable behavior in marriage? What is the line beyond which a person's behavior cannot go and still be conducive to a continued relationship? What is the breaking point in marriage?

The story of a sterling character of yesteryear who opted for divorce rather than disgrace may help us to find some answers to that question. Her name was Vashti. Her story is told in the book of Esther.

The book of Esther is known as the story of the queen who saved her people. Esther, who was a Jew, ascended to the throne at a strategic time which enabled her to save her fellow Jews from the tyranny of Haman. Read the book of Esther to see her intriguing story and her incomparable courage. Preliminary to the story of the queen who saved her people (Esther), however, was the story of the queen who saved her character (Vashti). Vashti was a sterling character who discovered that her husband was worse than she took him for. She arrived at a point in her marriage when she had to say, "Enough is enough. I will go no further."

The scene opens at a party hosted by Vashti's husband, King Ahasuerus. It was a real bash. The king's party would probably make one of Hugh Hefner's parties seem like a picnic at a Christian day school.

It was a party of drunken revelry. The Bible says, "Drinks were served in golden goblets, goblets of different kinds, and the royal wine was lavished according to the bounty of the king" (Esther 1:7, RSV).

Drinking is becoming increasingly popular in America today. A recent Gallup poll indicated that 71 percent of the adults surveyed said that they drink. A 1969 Gallup poll reported 64 percent said they were drinkers.[1] Those who declare alcohol's dangers are considered old-fashioned or straightlaced. The fact cannot be denied, however, that the consumption of alcoholic beverages is inevitably accompanied by problems.

The number of families troubled by a serious problem drinker is now up to 18 percent. Ann Landers says that alcoholism has ruined more marriages than anything else known to man. It is a lubricant for violence and a contributor to death on the highway. One doctor concluded that it affects every organ in the body except the kidneys, and he pointed out that cirrhosis is now the fifth leading death cause in America.[2]

The glamorous call to "go for all the gusto you can get" is a camouflage which hides the true outcome of alcoholism. More accurate is the description given by one man.

> We drank for happiness and became unhappy.
> We drank for joy and became miserable.
> We drank for sociability and became argumentative.
> We drank for sophistication and became obnoxious.
> We drank for friendship and made enemies.
> We drank for sleep and awakened without rest.
> We drank for strength and felt weak.
> We drank "medicinally" and acquired health problems.
> We drank for relaxation and got the shakes.
> We drank for bravery and became afraid.
> We drank for confidence and became doubtful.
> We drank to make conversation easier and slurred our speech.
> We drank to feel heavenly and ended up feeling like hell.
> We drank to forget and were forever haunted.
> We drank for freedom and became slaves.
> We drank to erase problems and saw them multiply.
> We drank to cope with life and invited death.[3]

Oblivious to the accompanying problems, King Ahasuerus served his guests all the liquor they could drink. As the liquor flowed, the artificial stimulation of the party increased, and the drunken revelry continued for seven days.

It was also a party of lustful experimentation. The Bible describes the context of the party: "couches of gold and silver on a mosaic pavement of porphyry, marble, mother-of-pearl and precious stones" (Esther 1:6, RSV). Then the Bible describes the character of the party: "The king had given orders to all the officials of his palace to do as every man desired" (v. 8, RSV).

For seven days the party continued. All sense of right and wrong was drowned in the heavy flow of liquor. Emotions reached a level of frenzy. Bored with the thrills that had been going on, the king decided to spice up the party with a special request. He sent orders to his queen, Vashti, to come before the guests so that they might behold her beauty.

Two alternatives were open to Vashti at that point. She could submit to her husband's request, become a spectacle at which the guests could lavish their lustful looks, and open herself to disgrace. Or she could refuse the request with the consequence of either being put to death or divorced. She could sacrifice her character for the sake of marriage, or she could sacrifice her marriage for the sake of character. Vashti made her choice. Character was more important than continued existence with a man who did not really care for her. She did not have to live with him, but she did have to live with herself. She came to a point where she decided that "enough was enough." She opted for divorce rather than the continuation of a meaningless relationship.

Many today stand where Vashti stood. They, too, are at the crossroads between disgrace or divorce, dissolution of a marriage or destruction of themselves. Should marriage be maintained, even at the cost of sacrificing character? Or should character be maintained, even at the cost of sacrificing marriage? When is enough, enough? Is divorce an option for the Christian today? Proper perspective is the key to answering these questions.

PERSPECTIVE ON DIVORCE

First, we need a proper perspective on divorce. The problem of divorce has mushroomed. Most statistics indicate that one in every three marriages will end in divorce. In the past some could piously claim, "We've never had a divorce in our family." Few can make that claim anymore, for so widespread has divorce become that no one seems to be immune. The pressure of social mores formerly made divorce acceptable only as a last resort. Social mores have changed, and now divorce is often accepted as the first resort. Why bother with a disagreeable partner when you can easily find another more agreeable one? Why try to rekindle an old flame when you can strike a new match? Such seems to be the prevailing attitude of our day.

What is the Christian to think? How is divorce to be evaluated from a Christian perspective? To answer such questions, the Christian turns to the Bible to see what God said about divorce in his Word. We are somewhat surprised to see that very little is said about divorce in the Bible. The word "divorce" appears only five times in the Bible (Jer. 3:8; Matt. 5:32; Lev. 21:14; 22:13; Num. 30:9). Another six references are made to a bill of divorcement (Deut. 24:1,3; Isa. 50:1; Matt. 5:31; 19:7; Mark 10:4).

Divorce was generally permitted in Old Testament times. Deuteronomy 24:1 says that divorce was permitted if a man found "some indecency" in his wife. Divorce was permitted at times for religious reasons (Ezra 10:3,44; Deut. 7:3). Childlessness was also at times a reason for divorce (Mal. 2:15). The only stated regulation was that a man who wished to divorce his wife must give her a bill of divorcement (Deut. 24:1-4).

In New Testament times, the divorce question was hotly

debated between the followers of Rabbi Shammai and the followers of Rabbi Hillel. The former accepted divorce only on the most serious grounds. The latter advocated divorce for even the flimsiest of reasons. If a wife burned her husband's supper, if she went about with her head uncovered, if she flirted with another man, if she were a noisy woman, or if her husband found a prettier woman, she could be tossed aside.

Hoping to gain Jesus' support for their side, the followers of Shammai and Hillel confronted Jesus with the issue. Jesus refused to take either side. Instead, he pointed out that divorce was not a part of God's original intent for mankind. Only man's "hardness of heart" made necessary the concession on divorce (Matt. 19:8).

The strongest condemnation of divorce comes in Malachi 2:16. The prophet condemned the Jews for putting aside the wives of their youth. He declared the sentiment of God, "For I hate divorce [sending away]." Before you assume too much from that statement, let me point out something I discovered.

Deuteronomy 16:22 says that the Lord hates setting up a sacred pillar, which is a reference to idolatry. That is, when you set up anything else in your life as your god, God hates it. That is the same Hebrew word for hate as is used in Malachi 2:16.

Amos 5:21 says that God even hated the feast days of Israel because they had corrupted them. That is, when you come to worship but do not worship God in a worthily way, God hates it. Again, the same Hebrew word.

Proverbs 6:16-19 says, "There are six things which the LORD hates,/Yes, seven which are an abomination to Him:/Haughty eyes, a lying tongue,/And hands that shed innocent blood,/A heart that devises wicked plans,/Feet that run rapidly to evil,/A false witness *who* utters lies,/And one who spreads strife among brothers." Once more the same word for *hate* is used.

Does God hate divorce? Yes, for it is a departure from his original intention for the home. Does God hate divorce more than he hates idolatry or lying or insincere worship or gossip or deception? Not according to the Bible. God hates every abominable act (Deut. 12:31), not just divorce.

Somehow we must gain that perspective. Divorce is not the primal sin of man. It is not the epitome of disobedience, nor is it the one failure for which we cannot be forgiven. It is simply another testimony to our humanity, another sign of our unwillingness to live up to God's ideal.

Cecil Osborne said it well when he declared, " 'Till death do us part' is a goal rather than a requirement."[4]

PERSPECTIVE ON MARRIAGE

In addition, we must be careful to maintain a proper perspective on marriage. A wedding ceremony is not a gateway that leads into a garden of uninterrupted bliss, even for a Christian. Conflict is an inevitable part of marriage. We need to accept that fact. We need to communicate that truth to our children.

I heard of a dentist who married a pedicurist. They fought tooth and toenail! Really, you don't have to be a dentist and pedicurist to experience the reality of conflict. All you have to be is married. Marriage is the meshing together of two lives into one. In such a process, conflict will inevitably arise. Several sensitive spots are most likely to provoke conflict in marriage.

Contrasting personal expectations is the primary source of conflict. Where do we learn about what to expect in marriage? Basically, there are three sources.

One source is the home in which we grew up. Our parents' model provided our first information on how a husband and a wife were to function. The problem with this source is that our parents were usually far from the ideal in their role modeling. In addition, many dimensions of their relationship remained hidden from us as children.

Another source is what we read and saw over the years. Movies, television, books—all of these fed our computer with ideas of what a husband and a wife are to do. One does not have to listen long to recognize the inadequacy of this source.

We also learn of marriage from our married friends. By watching them and talking to them, our expectations of marriage are shaped further. Since our friends do not always paint the picture as it is, this source, too, is inadequate.

From these three basic sources comes the input which is fed into our mental computer. The result is a certain understanding of roles and responsibilities in marriage. No two people have identical expectations because no two people have identical input. Marriage, then, is a daily adventure in which two people seek to bring their different personal expectations into some kind of correlation. Conflict often arises in that process.

In-laws can also be a source of conflict. Although this has been overstressed at times in the past, it can nevertheless be a real problem. Most in-law problems will not reach the level of one Chinese wife who told the court she had left her husband because her mother-in-law slept under the bed! Still, planning time with the two in-law families, scheduling holidays, and relating to them in the new way that marriage demands will often open the door for conflict.

Money is another primary source of conflict in the home. Someone has defined *incompatible* as the time when a husband loses his income and the wife is no longer "patible." John Drakeford reports that in one counseling center a study revealed that almost half of the people who came for marital counseling reported money problems. It was not that their income was inadequate. They simply could not agree on how to spend what they had.[5]

The *value systems* which each mate has also provide tension at times. Something as practical as deciding which church to go to can be a problem when the two individuals come from different denominational backgrounds. The question of values goes deeper than that. It involves a person's philosophy of life. One's philosophy of life, his understanding of what things are really important in life, will determine his life-style and his relationships. Settling in on a life-style compatible to both mates is not an easy task.

The *sexual* dimension of marriage is another area for problems. The Clinebells suggest that difficulty in sexual adjustment is more often the rule than the exception during the early years of marriage.[6] A study by Western Psychiatric Institute and Clinic in Pittsburg in 1978 indicated that even in happy marriages, both husbands and wives admit to some sexual problems.[7] Sexual compatibility is not automatic. It takes time. And the road that leads to it is not free of roadblocks and detours.

The point of all this is that there are sensitive spots in *every* marriage. Tension is a part of *every* relationship. Conflicts come to *every* couple. Perfect marriages exist only in fairy tales, not in real life. The idea that a tension-free marriage is possible is a myth. Truer to life is the summary of one man who said, "Many couples get divorces. The others fight it out to the end."

This proper perspective of marriage must be maintained. When problems come, accept them as a part of married life. When conflicts arise, don't check out on your marriage. Rather, try to work through your conflict to a deeper, more mature, more rewarding relationship. Remember that God's intention for marriage is for it to be a permanent, life-long relationship between one man and one woman. That is God's ideal, not a perfect marriage but a permanent marriage.

PROPER PERSPECTIVE ON THE BREAKING POINT

Only when this proper perspective on divorce and marriage has been declared can we move on to the question, When is enough, enough? Even then the question is not easy to answer. Let me offer some suggestions.

When abuse is advanced, that is enough. Physical and mental violence in the home, a problem of long standing, is now coming out of the closet. The extent of the problem is difficult to discern, but it is evidently widespread. One study suggests that at least four-and-one-half million women have been beaten by the men they love. Another estimate is that in 25 to 50 percent of all marriages, family violence occurs. Yet another report is that every eighteen seconds a woman is beaten by her husband or boyfriend. In our age of violence, even the home is not immune.

Attitudes toward physical abuse in the home have changed over the centuries. An ancient Egyptian proverb suggested, "Beat your wife. If you don't know a reason, she probably does."[8] Abigail Van Buren, in one of her "Dear Abby" columns, is closer to the modern-day evaluation of it when she wrote, "A man who beats a woman is sick. And a woman who sticks around for repeated beatings is sicker."

Why do women stay around even when abuse is advanced? One writer on the subject concisely capsules the situation:

> Battered women themselves often say that "love" and "the children" are their reasons. But love, common sense tells us, needs mutual respect to survive. And children are never helped by parents who fight violently. Experts on behavior

say the battered woman doesn't leave home because of her fear of change and the unknown, and her dependence, both financial and emotional.[9]

A husband who beats his wife needs to be helped if that is possible. If not, the wife has two choices. She can stay and take it. Or she can say, "Enough is enough. I'll go no further."

When commitment is challenged, that is enough. No relationship of life is to have priority over our relationship with God. Jesus made that clear in his declaration, "If anyone comes to Me, and does not hate his own father and mother and wife and children and brothers and sisters, yes, and even his own life, he cannot be My disciple" (Luke 14:26). Love for Christ is to come first.

This does not mean that in the give-and-take of marriage, one or the other of the partners will not be able to participate in their church life as they want to. It does mean that when a husband or a wife consistently demands that their mate do something contrary to the will of God, he/she will eventually have to take the step of Vashti and say, "Enough is enough. I will go no further."

When efforts have been exhausted, that is enough. Marriage is a relationship which demands participation by two people. Marriage at its best demands two people at their best who give their best. Some marriages reach the stage where one or both of the partners are no longer willing to give what it takes to make the marriage work.

R. Lofton Hudson gives some examples of such marriages:

those which (1) were simply bad choices in the first place— some people are so incompatible that they cannot stand each other; (2) two people slide into some kind of faulty and pathological relationship so that their staying together becomes untenable; (3) the cost of preserving the marriage becomes too high for one or both; (4) one, because of inner reasons, perhaps mental illness, even physical disability or unwillingness to live in the depriving situation, decides to leave the marriage; or (5) both feel that they do not find enough rewards in the marriage and therefore mutually agree to call it quits.[10]

Every effort needs to be expended to salvage such relationships from the marital junkyard. However, a couple may come to a point where nothing more can be done. The relationship is dead. At that point a divorce does not end the relationship. Divorce is merely the acknowledgement that the relationship has already ended.

CONCLUSION

"Till death do us part" is the goal God sets for marriage. The example of Vashti shows us, however, that when confronted by the choice between sacrificing character in order to save a marriage or sacrificing a marriage to save character, the latter may be the better way.

8
The Serving Single: *Anna*
Luke 2:36-38

I'll never forget Annie P. Morton. She was already over ninety years old when she joined our church and had been a widow for many years. Because she moved to our neighborhood to be near her son, she joined the church I pastored. In our first encounter she said, "Preacher, I don't want to just sit around. I want to teach a class of young ladies." She went on to explain that "young ladies" meant those around sixty or seventy. And teach them she did. Out of the richness of her life, she provided a depth of spiritual wisdom to those ladies. No one in the church prayed more fervently, attended more regularly, gave more freely, or served more beautifully than did Annie P.

She was a modern-day version of one of the most inspiring singles of the Bible, a woman by the name of Anna, whose fulfillment in life came from serving the Lord. Three brief verses tell her story. What a beautiful picture these verses paint.

There is a question about what the eighty-four years refers to (Luke 2:37). It could be that she was eighty-four years old. Other scholars suggest that the eighty-four refers to the length of her widowhood. If the latter is the case, she must have been over one hundred at the time she witnessed the dedication service of Jesus.

What did she do with her time? The Bible says, "She never left the temple, serving night and day with fastings and prayer." She was the forerunner of those singles today who declare, "We want to be the church too!"

Her life had not been an easy one. Like Naomi, Anna had lost her mate, apparently after only a short marriage of seven years. Rather than striking out at God because of her loss, Anna turned to him. Dedication rather than destruction was the ultimate outcome of her tragedy. She found her place in her religion.

Is there a place for the single in the church today? Can the single adult find fulfillment as a serving single? Certainly. Anna's experience provides some helpful direction.

SHE STUDIED

How did Anna find peace and fulfillment? The first factor evident in the picture painted of her is that she developed spiritually. Before you can give yourself away, you must have something to give. Before you can effectively serve the Lord, you have to apply to your life the spiritual disciplines that lead to growth. You have to develop yourself.

How can it happen?

Personal development begins when we *discover our gifts*. The Bible says that God has given every Christian (single as well as married) the ability to do certain things well. First Corinthians 12:7 says, "To each one is given the manifestation of the spirit." Ephesians 4:7 declares, "But to each one of us grace was given according to the measure of Christ's gift." In 1 Corinthians 7:7 Paul added, "However each man has his own gift from God." God has given to each of us a spiritual gift. The first order of business is to discover our gift or gifts.

Let me suggest some steps that will help you in your search.

You must start with awareness. Study the listings of spiritual gifts in the New Testament: 1 Corinthians 12; Romans 12; Ephesians 4; and 1 Peter 4. These lists are not exhaustive but are examples of the way God gifts individuals. A close study will reveal the possible gifts with which God can endow an individual Christian.

The next step is appeal. What do you enjoy doing? What are you good at? What is it that touches you and appeals to you to do something about? The revelation of God's will is not always spectacular, nor will God's purpose for you be repulsive. Rather, God often reveals his will in the normal commonsense experiences of life through the things that appeal to you.

A third step is asking. Prayer needs to be a central part of the search. James 4:2 suggests, "Ye have not because ye ask not" (KJV). Prayer is a vital tool in discovering your spiritual gift.

Association is another important step. One of the most marvelous benefits of Christian fellowship is that someone often sees something in us which we do not see in ourselves. Rufus Jones called this "finding the life cue." In our association with others, very often they will find the life cue in our lives or draw it out. By so doing, they help us to discover our gift.

Because of an overloaded schedule, one pastor asked a Sunday School teacher to help him counsel some young couples. The teacher sensed this as her life cue. She enrolled in a therapy course. After two years she had progressed so much that she was asked to join the hospital staff. How did she discover her gift? Through association with another Christian.

What do you do when you have discovered your gift? The next stage is to *develop your gift.* Special reading, practical experience, formal education, and volunteer service may all be part of the developmental process.

The third and most vital stage is to *dedicate your gift.* Put it into action. Many people spend so much time in the search that they never get to the service. Not so with Anna. Her life reflected a deep, personal dedication to God. She used her gift in the service of God.

The discovery, development, and dedication of your gift is only part of your personal preparation for service to God. Another part is to prepare yourself spiritually to use 'that gift. This is what Paul said to the Ephesian Christians. "And He gave some as apostles, and some as prophets, and some as evangelists, and some as pastors and teachers, for the equipping of the saints for the work of service, to the building up of the body of Christ" (Eph. 4:11-12). This is the idea of gifts. But notice also how Paul combined with this the idea of personal spiritual development: "until we all attain to the unity of the faith, and of the knowledge of the Son of God, to a mature man, to the measure of the stature which belongs to the fulness of Christ" (v. 13). Each of us as Christians, single or married, is to "grow up in all aspects into Him, who is the head, even Christ" (v. 15).

The message of the New Testament is that salvation for the Christian is both a once-for-all event and a lifelong process. The Christian life is pictured as a building in the process of being built, a race in the process of being run, a spiritual self in the process of being developed. It is not enough to be born again. We must practice the disciplines that lead to growth.

How do we experience this growth? What does it take to develop personally into the kind of individual who can properly use his gifts for the benefit of God's kingdom? In the New Testament, we have several models.

In 2 Corinthians 3:18 we have the *concentration model.* "But we all, with unveiled face beholding as in a mirror the glory of the Lord, are being transformed into the same image from glory to glory." How are we transformed into the image of Christ? By beholding the glory of the Lord with unveiled face. This means to concentrate on Jesus Christ in our thought life, to concentrate on him in our reading, to concentrate on him in the company we keep, to concentrate on him by participation in worship and personal study. E. Stanley Jones was right when he said, "The process of Christian maturity is the process of the redemption of the imagination—redeeming it from self-concentration, past-failure concentration, sin-concentration—and concentrating it on 'The Lord.' "[1]

In 2 Peter 1:5-8 we have the *addition model.*

> For this very reason make every effort to supplement your faith with virtue, and virtue with knowledge, and knowledge with self-control, and self-control with steadfastness, and steadfastness with godliness, and godliness with brotherly affection, and brotherly affection with love. For if these things are yours and abound, they keep you from being ineffective or unfruitful in the knowledge of our Lord Jesus Christ (RSV).

How are we made fruitful and effective in our Christian lives? By adding each of these elements to the other in our life.

You begin with faith. Belief in Christ as your Lord is the foundation for growth. Add to that moral excellence or purity. Purity leads to spiritual growth for as Jesus said, it is the pure in heart who shall see God (Matt. 5:8). "Then," said Peter, "add knowledge." The Greek word means insight or understanding. The only way to grow as a Christian is to grow in our knowledge of the Lord. The only way we can grow in knowledge is to study. Next, add *discipline.* This word is often translated *temperance* but more literally means "self-control." This is the discipline Jesus had in mind in Mark 9:43 when he said that anything which offends God or deters us in our Christian life should be put away.

The next factor to add is *perseverance.* This Greek word is often translated "patience." Literally it means "to

remain under the load" and carries the idea of perseverance rather than patience. Persistence, stick-to-activity,
consistency—all of these are elements of the word. The
key to growth is a consistent commitment. Then Peter said
to add godliness. I believe he was referring to that feeling
of fellowship, that quality of oneness that comes through
prayer. The last two ingredients to add to our lives are
brotherly kindness and Christian love. The secret here is
that as we open ourselves to others through genuine concern and share our lives with them this will create growth
in our own lives.

Personal spiritual development comes through an addition of these essential ingredients to our foundation of
faith.

In Hebrews 12:1 we have the *subtraction model.*
"Therefore, since we have so great a cloud of witnesses
surrounding us, let us also lay aside every encumbrance,
and the sin which so easily entangles us, and let us run
with endurance the race that is set before us."

Growth comes not only by adding things to our lives but
also by subtracting things from our lives. We are to subtract every "encumbrance" and "sin." The word "encumbrance" does not carry a moral connotation. It does
not mean something evil but something superfluous. It is
an unnecessary burden that prevents us from running at
full speed. Some habits, some relationships, some pas-
times may not be evil but they may be superfluous and
unnecessary for the Christian. In such a case they are
merely excess baggage that prevent you from full development in your life. They need to be discarded.

The word "sin," of course, does carry a moral connotation. It means those things that are evil. It may be vulgar
sin like sexual impurity or polished sin like pride; it may be
a sin of action or a sin of attitude. Of whichever variety,
these sins need to be cast off, subtracted from our lives, so

that we can move with full speed toward the fulfillment of the purpose God has for our lives.

Personal spiritual development comes by subtracting from our lives those ingredients which weight us down spiritually and morally.

In 1 Corinthians 3:11-13 we have the *construction model*.

> For no man can lay a foundation other than the one which is laid, which is Jesus Christ. Now if any man builds upon the foundation with gold, silver, precious stones, wood, hay, straw, each man's work will become evident; for the day will show it, because it is to be revealed with fire; and the fire itself will test the quality of each man's work.

As Christians we are alike in our foundation. We are not alike, however, in our fruit. The difference between a Christian who is mature and productive and one who is immature and fruitless is determined by the material with which we build our lives. Each act, each word, each relationship, each thought is like a stone which we place upon the foundation which Christ has given to us. Personal spiritual development comes when we use the permanent, imperishable material of Christlike actions and attitudes to build on our foundation of faith.

We don't know what model Anna used. Perhaps she used all of them. The finished product is all that we have presented to us. Her life was characterized by "fastings and prayer." Through study, she had developed herself personally into an individual God could use.

SHE SERVED

Look again at Anna and you will discover that she was not a person whose only concern was to discover and develop her spiritual gifts, whose only desire was to develop herself. Instead, we see in Anna a single who dedicated herself to God in service. There was not a special single-again class for her in the Temple. Nor did they have a single adult rabbi to deal with her needs. She nevertheless found her niche and poured out her life in service to God.

So can the single of today. More than ever before singles have an opportunity to be the church too. An awareness of the single adult population, their unique problems, and their untapped potential is apparent in the church today.

Singles were a special part of the ministry at the church I pastored in Dallas, Texas. They taught in our Sunday School. They worked in our choir program. They served on all the vital committees of the church. They ushered. They made up almost half of the adult choir. They supported the church with their tithes. When I left, a single adult was placed on the pulpit committee. Their service was vital to the life of the church. There is also a growing singles program in the First Baptist Church of Pensacola, Florida. In both churches singles are discovering the joy of service.

David is an excellent example. As a young single, David had a deep desire to serve. He became the teacher of our twelfth-grade boys' class. They were a tough group, a real challenge. Through his dedication and genuine concern, David reached those boys. He had them over to his apartment. He took them to ball games. He went out to eat with them. He went camping with them. He listened to their problems and offered wise spiritual counsel. He served God in a magnificent way.

David is a living testimony that, as a single, a person can serve effectively in the church today. Yet, the fact is that singles are often left out of the church. Why? The problem can be on either side.

It could be that the church is not prepared for a ministry to singles. In fact, many churches are not even aware of the need of such a ministry. It has been correctly stated, "Many churches neglect singles not because they plan to but because they do not plan not to."

Britton Wood's book entitled *Single Adults Want to Be the Church, Too* is one of the most comprehensive guides I have seen for starting and growing a ministry to single adults. It is a manual every concerned pastor should use to create single awareness in his church. In a day when one out of every three adults in America is single, we dare not miss this crucial ministry challenge.[2]

At times, however, the problem is not with the church. The problem could be on the side of the single. "They won't accept me at that church" could be not so much a description of the church's attitude as it is a projection of the attitude of the single adult. At times, it is a single's cop-out for avoiding the challenge of church involvement. At other times, it is simply a misconception.

Do you as a single want to be the church too? If you have been frustrated in your attempts, would you like to discover where the real problem is? Then, take the following steps.

Do an attitude check. Check your attitude toward yourself. Have you accepted your own self-worth as a single? Is your singleness making you better or bitter? Linda Lawson, in her book *Life As a Single Adult,* said, "I am committed to the belief that a person can be happy and single, be growing and single, be loving and loved and single."[3] Have you made that discovery?

Then check your attitude toward others. Do you resent others because of their "coupleness"? Do you feel yourself left out, or are you able to count your single blessings? Do you enjoy the company of other singles, or have you withdrawn from life? Perhaps your frustration about church involvement is merely a reflection of your envy or isolationism.

Your attitude toward God also needs to be checked. Is your stance more accurately positionized by the question, "Why me, Lord?" or by the statement of Paul, "For I have learned to be content in whatever circumstances I am" (Phil. 4:11).

Check your attitude toward the church. Overcoming a negative attitude toward the church may be the first step in finding a productive involvement in God's work. Is your evaluation of the church a true evaluation of today or a caricature of the past? Just because church was boring when you were a teenager does not mean that it is boring today. Just because the church in which you were raised had a negative attitude toward singles does not mean that the churches where you live now have that same negative attitude. If you would attend church with an open mind, setting aside your preconceived notions about the church, you may be surprised at the warmth, excitement, and fellowship that is a part of today's church.

A second step is to *attend church.* If you live in a city, a large number of churches can be reached in a matter of minutes. Find out what is going on in the churches. Look for churches that already have an active singles group. It may take several visits, but stay after it.

A third step is to *make yourself available.* It could be that you will have to form the nucleus of a singles' group yourself. The church may be ready, but they may need someone to spearhead the new ministry to singles. Make an appointment with the pastor to talk about your desires and needs. If there is a multistaff, talk to the one in the area where you would like to get plugged in. Look for a job that needs to be done and then volunteer. Single or married, few churches will turn down volunteers who express a genuine desire to serve.

It may be a slow process that demands patience on your part. And you may be occasionally rebuffed. Nevertheless, if you will persist with a consistent commitment you like Anna, can find your niche and pour out your life ir service to God.

SHE SHARED

There is more to this picture of Anna. If you are tempted to categorize Anna as a cloistered individual who lived a monastic life, simply developing herself and carrying out her service in the church, then you need to look at her story again. When she saw the Messiah, Anna immediately began to spread the good news to the people of the city. Actually, the Bible says that she "continued to speak of Him to all those who were looking for the redemption of Jerusalem" (Luke 2:38).

In his second letter to the Corinthians, Paul described the process of reconciliation which was brought about through Christ. Jesus Christ reconciled us, that is, he brought us together with God. Then, Paul added that God has given to us the ministry of reconciliation (2 Cor. 5:18). "Therefore, we are ambassadors for Christ, as though God were entreating through us" (v. 20).

Has it ever dawned on you as a single that this verse applies to you in the same way it applies to married adults? All of us are God's ambassadors. We are his representatives in the world. In international life an ambassador is put in a place where he can most effectively communicate with the people and is best equipped to do so. Do you think that perhaps God wants to follow the same methodology in the spiritual realm? A Christian doctor can probably reach another doctor for Christ more effectively than can anyone else. A Christian coach can best impress a coach with the claims of Christ. Why? Because they talk the same language. They understand each other. They speak out of the same life context.

Who can better reach singles for Christ than other singles? Our minister to single adults in one church I pastored was divorced. This experience gave him a common life context with the very people he was trying to reach. When he sat down with a divorced person and said, "I know what you are going through," he really did. He had been there. He spoke their language; he understood them.

One out of every three adults today is single. Who will reach these singles for Christ? Who, if not other singles who have dedicated themselves to the service of Christ and are willing to share with other singles the difference Christ can make in their lives?

Several years ago I pastored in Atlanta, Georgia. I went by one day to visit a lady who had sent her child to our Mother's Day Out program. I wanted to talk to her about the Lord and seek to involve her in our church. She and I had been visiting only a few minutes when her husband came home from work. As he walked into the room, she stood up and said, "Honey, this is the pastor from the Woodland Hills Baptist Church. He came to talk to you about God." Then she walked out of the room.

Rather awkwardly, we sat down and began to talk. It was as if a dam broke and all of the desires and needs and hurts of his soul came pouring out. For over an hour he talked about what he was and what he wanted to be. He talked about his needs, about his emptiness, about his hunger, about his fears. When he had talked himself out, I shared with him how Christ could meet his need. That afternoon, we kneeled in his living room as he invited Christ to come into his heart.

I have had many other experiences like that over the years. The factor that made this particular experience stick in my mind was what the man said right before I left his house. "Preacher," he said, "I have been waiting five years for someone to help me get straightened out with God.''

All around you are singles whose greatest need is to have someone who will help them get straightened out with God. If you won't do it, who will?

9
The Sensational Single: *John*
John 1:6-9, 15-37

In John 1:6, interjected rather abruptly into this exalted description of the eternal Word, who became flesh in Jesus Christ, is the introduction of a historical character by the name of John. In all of the Gospels we see a close relationship and a striking similarity between these two figures, Jesus and John.

Both had a common ancestry, historically speaking. Both lived short but strenuous lives. Both saw the initial sunny skies of enthusiastic support replaced by the thunderous clouds of hatred. Both preached about the kingdom of God. Both experienced cruel and undeserved deaths. Both had a little handful of disciples who remained loyal to them. Jesus and John were very much alike.

There was also an inescapable difference between the two, and we see it in the verbs John used for each in the first chapter of this Gospel. In verse 1, about Jesus, the Gospel writer declared, "In the beginning was the Word." He used the verb *en,* which expressed continuous existence. This verb attributes to Jesus timeless, uncreated existence. It means that there never was a time when he did not exist. In verse 6, about the Baptizer, John said, "There came a man, sent from God, whose name was John." Here he used the verb *egeneto,* which means "to become." The verb in verse 6 speaks of John's beginning as a beginning in time. It refers to the coming into being of something that was previously nonexistent.[1]

All of the Gospels emphasize this difference. All are emphatic that John the Baptizer was not the Messiah, not Elijah returned (Mal. 4:5-6), not the prophet spoken of in Moses' day (Deut. 18:18), not the light of the world, not the divine Logos, but simply a voice in the wilderness preparing the way for the Lord. In comparison with Jesus, John's importance is always minimized.

When he is compared with other men, however, John is exalted. One of the clearest expressions of this is in Luke 7:28 where Jesus says, "Among those born of women none is greater than John" (RSV). Apart from Jesus there is no other individual in all of the Gospels who is painted with such glorious brush strokes as is this one who came to prepare the world for the incarnation of the divine Logos.

What we often fail to note is that John was single. Both the nature of his ministry and the lack of any mention of a wife imply that John did not have a wife. His was a dangerous, distinct mission from God. He was "set apart" for that special mission. He would allow nothing to hold him back from the fulfillment of God's assigned purpose for him.

What was it about John's life that made him so sensational? Over 140 verses in the four Gospels tell the full story about him. Out of all this material I want to paint a portrait of this sensational single of the past. What kind of man was this about whom Jesus could say, "Among those born of women none is greater than John"?

A CALLED MAN

First, we see that the Baptizer was a called man. Verse 6 says that he was sent from God. The word used here *(apestalmenos)* is the same word used in verse 19 when the writer of the Fourth Gospel says the Jews sent priests and Levites from Jerusalem to find out about this unique wilderness preacher. It is the same word used in John 3:34 where the writer says that Jesus was sent from God to bring life into the world of death.

What does "sent from God" mean? It means commissioned. It means called. It means a special person sent to a special place at a special time to carry out a special mission. When the author of the Fourth Gospel described John in this way, he was putting him in the same category as Moses (Ex. 3:10,15), as the prophets (Isa. 6:8), and even as Jesus himself (John 3:17), who were all sent from God.

John's significance derives from the fact that he had been called to carry out a certain task. John was called to be the clasp between the two covenants, the last of the prophets and the first of the Christian era. The power and popularity and permanent influence that John enjoyed are found not in any unique ability with which he was endowed but in the fact that he responded obediently to God's plan and purpose for his life. The significance of John is that he discovered God's will for him and committed himself to doing it. He said yes to God's call.

The message underlying this needs to be clearly stated: God has a task for every man and a man for every task. God has a distinct destiny for each of us. There will be no joy in our lives apart from doing that task God gives us.

In every generation God has been matching the task with the man and the man with the task. When there was a new start to be made after the Flood, there was Noah. When there was a nation to be established, there was Abraham. When there was a people to be delivered, there was Moses. When there was a Temple to be built, there was Solomon. When there was a Messiah to be proclaimed, there was John. When there was a world to be evangelized, there was Paul.[2]

God has a task to which he has called us. Be that task large or small, temporary or permanent, public or private, our only significance, our only joy, and our only glory will be found in discovering what that task is and committing ourselves to doing it. Your marital status has nothing to do with whether God has a task for you. Like a beautiful mosaic, Christ wants to piece together all of us—married and single—into a beautiful design.

John was a called man who responded obediently to that call.

A CLEAN MAN

John was also a clean man. Luke 1:15 and Matthew 11:18 indicate that John was a Nazarite. A Nazarite was one who refrained from wine and unclean food, who refused to make contact with dead bodies, who refused to have his hair cut. The purpose of the Nazarite vow was to enable an individual to remain free from the worldly forces of society, to remain pure, so that he could more effectively carry out a certain task for God.

John was called by God to perform a certain task in the world—to prepare the way for the Lord. John was so determined to do it in the best possible way that he refrained from any outside influence that might hurt him. He remained clean so he could carry out his call.

Again, there is a message here for us. We are living today in a world filled with contaminating forces. Temptation is on every hand. The other day I heard about a man who was told by his doctor that if he didn't quit drinking he would lose his hearing. The man said that he liked what he was drinking so much better than what he was hearing that he would not quit.

That is the kind of world we live in. What things we are hearing today! In this kind of world it would be easy to get caught up in the whirlwind of worldliness and forget who we are, to yield to the temptation of the world and be like everyone else, to become brainwashed by the lures of immorality and forget the demand of holiness. How we need to remember that impurity defuses our spiritual power.

Several months ago my wife greeted my return home with a distress signal. "The vacuum cleaner doesn't work," she said. "See if you can fix it." The reason her request was so distressful is that my mechanical ability on a range from one to ten would be rated minus three.

I approached the vacuum cleaner with anxious uncertainty. I looked it all over. I turned it on. It sounded all right, but it wouldn't pick anything up. I removed the arm and put it to my eye. No light shined through from the other end. Eureka! Being the mechanical genius that I am, I reached a conclusion. Something was clogging up the arm. With a broomstick, I removed the guilty culprit, a big clump of lint and dirt. Now, the vacuum cleaner worked fine.

Do you hear the message? Too much dirt can gum up the works and block off the power.

During the Korean conflict General Dean was captured and executed. He was given only a few short minutes to write a letter to his family before being shot. He wrote only eight or nine lines, and in the heart of his message was a word to his son Bill. "Tell Bill," he wrote, "that the word is integrity."[3]

The word is still *integrity!* I don't care what the world says; I don't care how good the new morality sounds; neither does it matter what everyone else is doing. In our world which is reveling in excesses, rollicking in pleasure, reeling in drunkenness, revolting in morals, and rotting in sin, we who are called of God must keep ourselves clean so we can carry out our God given tasks.

A CHALLENGING MAN

John was also a challenging man. He was a man with a message, and there was no mistake about what he meant. It was all very clear. The message that he sent reverberating across the land had three basic points.

John said that the kingdom of God was at hand. How long had Israel waited for God's kingdom? A thousand years? Two thousand? When Abraham left his homeland with the promise of God in his heart, he thought that the promise would be fulfilled in his lifetime. But it wasn't. The Israelites had hoped for its fulfillment after their glorious deliverance from Egypt, but soon they were longing for something better than wilderness hardships and the pie in the sky by and by. The Israelites hoped for a place in the sun when they got their first king. When he failed, they hoped David would be the one, then David's son. And then the hope seems to have turned into a vague dream, postponed to some unknown future. Someday, they thought, God's kingdom would come.

The Jews wandered in Babylonian Exile with this hope in their hearts. They returned home and rebuilt the city of Jerusalem with this hope in their hearts. They fought the royal Romans under the leadership of the Maccabeans with this hope in their hearts. Someday, they believed, God would send a new king, a Messiah, who would establish God's kingdom on earth. Then suddenly, a man appeared in the wilderness to proclaim that the kingdom of God had come. Every Israelite could identify with and glorify in the first point of John's message.

The second part of his message jarred them. Because the kingdom of God had come, John said, the judgment of God was upon every man. The Jews didn't expect this.

They thought that when the kingdom came the Gentiles would be judged but the Israelites would be exalted to a position of leadership. On the contrary, John pointed out that they had sinned against almighty God just like the Gentiles and that all men were under God's judgment.

The third part of John's message was to repent and be baptized. Repentance is an act of the will by which a person decides that his ways are hurtful to God and he determines to turn from them. It doesn't mean to withdraw from the world. It means to live differently in the world. They would live for God. That brings insulation, not isolation.

The kingdom of God is at hand. The judgment of God is on every man. Thus, everyone should repent and turn back to God. That was John's message. And so convincing was he in proclaiming that message that all of Judea came out to hear him. Even the Sanhedrin sent a committee to investigate what was going on.

What is a single to do? How often that question is asked. Here is one answer to that perturbing question. Share your faith with others. By the deeds of your life and the declaration of your lips, proclaim the good news of God brought to us by Jesus Christ.

We need to just as clearly and just as convincingly proclaim this message to the world today. Man is a sinner. And the only response of sinful man to a holy God is to repent and to get right with him.

A COURAGEOUS MAN

Another evident characteristic of John was his courage. John would not be silent when confronted by sin, even if it were the king who was guilty. We often say that silence is golden. More often it is just plain yellow. But there was no yellow streak down John's back. He had a mission to carry out for God, and he would not let anybody or anything stand in his way. As one man expressed it: "John would rather be without a head than without a conscience." He was a man of courage.

A CONSUMED MAN

Jesus' reference to the Baptizer in John 5:35 reveals further that John was a consumed man. Jesus called John a burning and shining lamp.

Notice that he did not simply say that John was a burning lamp—heat without illumination. Nor did he say John was a shining lamp—illumination without heat. He said that John was a burning and shining lamp. What that means is that in order to shine for God, John had to burn for God. He was on fire for God.

The other day I heard someone called a fiery leader and then the person explained what he meant—the man had been fired three times. That is not what I mean about John. I mean that he was consumed with God. He was willing to expend all of his energies and all of his efforts for God.

Let me tell you what this means for us. It means that before we can shine for God we have to be willing to burn for God. A lot of people want to shine for God. There is not a Christian alive who at one time or another has not wanted to shine for Christ. Singles say, "We want to be the church too" or "We want to be an important part of God's kingdom." That's great! But there is a catch. The reason some Christians shine and others don't is not because some are married and others are single. That is immaterial. The difference is that, married or single, some are willing to pay the price and expend the energy and be consumed in their commitment to the cause of Christ, and others are not. John was. He was consumed for God's plan for his life. That was the secret of his life.

A CONTENTED MAN

In addition to all the other, John was a contented man. John was willing to give way to Jesus; he was willing for his disciples to follow Jesus. He was willing for Jesus to get the glory because he recognized who he was and what he was to do and he was content with it.

The other night I had to talk with the operator to make a long-distance call. She connected me with the party I wanted to talk to, then she went off the line. She didn't listen to what I said to the other party nor did she participate in the conversation. She did her job. Then she got out of the way. That is what John did. He connected people with the Lamb of God who takes away the sins of the world and then he just faded out.

Envy is a symptom of a lack of appreciation for our own self-worth. But there was no hint of jealousy, no shadow of envy in John. He knew what he was here for. He didn't care about trying to be more or less than what God called him to be. He was content being himself.

What a glorious character John the Baptist was—a man of courage and strength, a man in tune with God, a man consumed with God's purpose, a man obsessed with the light when other men were willing to live in the shadows, a single who used his singleness creatively to serve God.

10
The Surprised Single:
The Samaritan Woman
John 4

The story goes that competition was keen between a brother and sister, both quite wealthy, who tried to outdo each other in giving an expensive, unique gift to their grandmother for Christmas. One year the brother decided he would give it his best shot. So he bought a Zirkay bird, an exotic animal which could speak three languages and sing four different operatic arias. It cost him fifteen thousand dollars. With a note attached, which said, "I hope you enjoy it," he sent the bird to his grandmother. On the day after Christmas he called his grandmother. "How did you like the bird?" he asked the sweet little lady.

She responded, "It was delicious." Was he ever surprised!

In John 4 we see another person who was surprised. This story is one of the most magnificent examples of Jesus' concern for individuals. His Sermon on the Mount taught to the multitudes (Matt. 5—7), his Great Commission given to the delegation of disciples (Matt. 28:19-20), his parables proclaimed to the throngs of people (Matt. 13), all of these are important. If you really want to get to know Jesus, however, you need to study those intimate, isolated incidents in which he confronted individuals, person-to-person.

This is what John described in Jesus' encounter with the Samaritan woman at the well at Sychar. We'll call her

"Sally." Sally was a single, a fact which comes out as the story unfolds.

On the way to Galilee, Jesus and his disciples had to pass through Samaria. When they arrived at the well at Sychar, it was lunchtime. Jesus remained at the well to rest while the disciples went into town to buy food. While Jesus was waiting for the disciples to return, a Samaritan woman approached the well to draw water. When the disciples returned and found Jesus talking to this woman, they were surprised (v. 27). There were several reasons the disciples were surprised to find Jesus talking to her.

To begin with, she was a Samaritan and Jesus was a Jew. Between these two people there was no contact at all. So intense was the disfavor of the Jews toward the Samaritans that if the shadow of a Samaritan fell across a Jew he would consider himself contaminated. John's statement in verse 9 is a classic example of understatement, "For Jews have no dealings with the Samaritans."

In addition, this was a Samaritan woman. According to the customs of the day, it was not proper for a man to speak to a strange woman in public. It simply was not done.

Another factor was the character of the woman. It was in the heat of the day when the Samaritan woman came to the well. This was not the accustomed time to draw water. Women would come to the well in the early morning or late evening hours when it was cool. Why did this woman come in the middle of the day? Evidently, she was a woman of loose morals and questionable character who had been shunned by the other women of the city. To avoid their condemnation, she came at a time when she knew they would not be there. Jesus understood all of this and thus knew what kind of woman she was.

Add to all of these reasons the fact that Jesus was tired.

A great distance had already been covered on that day. It was hot and dusty. Jesus had nothing to eat or drink. What he needed most was some rest.

There were many reasons why Jesus would not have spoken to this strange, sinful Samaritan woman who was at the well of Sychar that day. Thus, not only the disciples but also the woman herself were surprised when Jesus initiated a conversation with her.

As Jesus talked with the woman, he surprised her even further by what he said. Jesus dealt with two dimensions of her life in which she experienced some real problems.

HER SPIRITUAL LIFE

Even a cursory reading of the story will reveal that this woman had some real spiritual problems. All of her life she had evidently felt something lacking in her life. Her knowledge of religion indicates that she had tried to meet that need through a life of faith. She was familiar with the patriarchs of the faith (v. 12), she knew about the prophets (v. 19), she was aware of the debate about the proper center for the worship of God (v. 20), and she was knowledgeable about the messianic expectations of the Hebrew people (v. 25). How long she had pursued this religious study or what drew her away from it we cannot tell. She knew enough about religion to be aware of the spiritual questions, but she did not know enough to realize the answers.

Not being able to satisfy her soul-hunger with religion, she then tried to satisfy the thirst in her soul by yielding to her passions. She went from one man to another and was at that time living with a man to whom she was not married. She had sunk so low that she no longer went through the motions of an official marriage relationship. She was similar to one lady of recent vintage who had been married so many times that she had rice marks on her face. A comedian told recently of another lady who had a wash and wear wedding gown! The fact that Sally the Samaritan had gone from one man to another indicates that this, too, had been a dead-end street.

Jesus saw her that day as a spiritually starved individual. He talked with her first of all about the gift of salvation that could quench her spiritual thirst and meet the need in her soul. He talked to her that day because she needed him.

Why do we need Jesus? Because we so often mess up our lives. If you have ever despaired of being the kind of person you don't want to be, if you have ever faced a situation that was quite beyond your powers to cope with, if you have ever cried yourself to sleep at night because of something you have done, then you know what it means to need Jesus. We need release from our guilt, forgiveness for our sins, and an opportunity to start over again. This comes only from Jesus.

We also need Jesus to give direction and purpose to our lives. This is the preventive power of Christianity. You don't have to have a messed up life to need Jesus. If you will allow his way of life to be your ideal and his presence in your life the motivating power then you can perhaps avoid the pitfalls of life into which so many people fall. Gypsy Smith, an evangelist of old, used to say that a hedge on the edge of the precipice was better than a hospital at the bottom. Jesus is more than a hospital at the bottom. He is a hedge at the top which will keep you from going over the edge. That is why we need Jesus.

We also need Jesus to fill our lives. The good news, Jesus said, is this: "I came that they might have life, and might have it abundantly" (John 10:10). Jesus will not subtract from your life. Rather, he will add to it. He will not restrict you but will set you free to enjoy life to its fullest.

What will this abundant life be like? I can only give you some general outlines. It will involve a gradually growing awareness of fellowship with the God of the universe. Abundant life will permeate your being with a peace of mind which will enable you to withstand the onslaught of inward doubts and outward difficulties. It will bring into your life a new power over temptations, a power that will enable you to accomplish what you could not accomplish on your own. It will bring a gradually increasing joy in your life. It will lead you to a deeper understanding of the meaning and purpose of life. It will lead you eventually to be able to stand at the end of life and say like Paul, "I have fought the good fight, I have finished the course, I have kept the faith; in the future there is laid up for me the crown of righteousness, which the Lord, the righteous Judge, will award to me on that day; and not only to me, but also to all who have loved His appearing" (2 Tim. 4:7-8).

I cannot completely describe how the abundant life will work itself out for you because we are all different. I am sure of this much however. Although it does not come all at once, this experience of abundant living begins when you, like Sally the Samaritan, turn your life over to Jesus Christ.

Some separate people into two categories—the good guys who are the Christians and the bad guys who are non-Christians. In my opinion that's not right. There aren't any good guys and bad guys. Instead, there are the bad ones who know it and the bad ones who don't know it.

When Sally approached the well that day she was a bad one who didn't know it. Before Jesus was through with her, she was a bad one who did know it and who found in him the answer to her deepest needs.

Sally, the Samaritan single, was surprised by the Savior because he touched the sensitive spot which was the key to her confused, empty life. He led her through the doorway to abundant life. Having dealt with her primary problem, Jesus then dealt with another dimension of her life.

HER SEX LIFE

Sally was even more surprised when Jesus began to talk to her about her sex life. When the Master asked her to bring her husband to the well (vv. 16-18), he brought her face to face with the sexual misbehavior of her life. For her, sex was not the sacred, special union of two lives as one that God intended it to be. Instead, she had abused sex. Having gone through five husbands, she was now living with a man to whom she was not even married. That sounds thoroughly modern, doesn't it? Someone has suggested that the old-fashioned couples today are not the ones who stay married but the ones who get married in the first place!

The implication of the encounter between Jesus and Sally was that the sexual dimension of her life would have to be brought in line with her spiritual commitment.

What about sex and the single today? Although the "swinging single" stereotype does not fit comfortably on all singles, studies reveal that singles are more sexually active today than in the past.

In our sexually explosive day, how does a single deal with the sex question? There are several options open to the single.

One alternative is *promiscuity*. Fannie Fling is a good example. The sex life was one part of her former marriage which had been fulfilling and satisfying to her. She missed the closeness, warmth, and pleasure of the sexual relationship. To fill the void she began a liberated sex life that led from one partner to another. Instead of fulfillment, however, she felt an increasing uncertainty about her new lifestyle.

Her mistake was that she did not realize the true dimensions of sex. Following the *Playboy* philosophy, she conceived of sex as a biological hunger, a purely physical experience. Sex in human life is much more than that. It is not just physical. It is also emotional, psychological, and relational. A purely physical relationship which does not also carry with it emotional involvement is a myth.

The mind is also involved. Like all behavior, sexual behavior is under the direction of the mind. As one man has said it, the primary sex organ for the human is the brain.

The sexual dimension in man is also relational. Ken Chafin sounds a healthy note when he suggests, "The emphasis most of us need to hear is that it is not the sex act which gives meaning to our relationship but it is the quality of the relationship which gives meaning to the sex act."[1]

Promiscuity is not a viable option for the Christian, then, because it neglects the emotional, psychological, and relational aspects of sex.

Another alternative suggested and tried today is *temporary liaisons.* This differs from promiscuity in that it is more selective and is usually experienced in the context of a "meaningful relationship" with another person. This alternative more closely approaches the experience of Sally. She was "living with a man" in a temporary relationship.

Apart from the strict biblical injunction against such sexual relationships outside of marriage, there are some very practical reasons why even these temporary liaisons in the context of a "meaningful relationship" are still inadequate.

In marriage the experiences of the total person are brought into the sex act. The couple will share all aspects of their lives with each other, experiences of the day, plans for the future, details about the house, decisions about the children. This totality of sharing enriches the sex act.

The marriage relationship also provides a permanence in which growth and maturation in sex can be experienced. The permanence allows trust to grow, and trust provides the freedom to experiment and develop within the marriage.

Marriage also provides a continuing context for sex. When the couple is older, and each is perhaps less physically appealing, sex still has meaning because it is fed by the rich memories of the years.

The exclusive commitment of marriage also removes the tension of competition. The fear of performing adequately enough to outdo someone else can create the tension which may produce frigidity or impotence. Within the context of marriage the exclusiveness prevents such fear.

Within marriage there is more likelihood that sex will be kept in its proper perspective. The ego challenge of a temporary relationship may cause sex to be exalted as more important than it really is. An imbalanced relationship can result. In marriage, sex is seen as one of many dimensions of the relationship. This leads to balance.

Sex within marriage is also free from the shadow of guilt. There are no questions to probe the consciences of a husband or a wife when they wake up the next morning. They know who they are and what their relationship is. Not so with those who have only an "understanding." Questions about the rightness of the relationship not affirmed by an official commitment of marriage will inevitably arise.[2]

That is why God limited full sexual expression to the permanent relationship between a husband and a wife. Not because God thought sex unimportant or because he wanted to deprive man of pleasure, but because sex was so vital that God wanted us to experience it only at its absolute best!

Then what other alternative is there for the single who wants to live in the favor of God? The biblical answer is *continence,* or as one woman labels it, "relinquishment."[3] This appears to be the acceptable alternative for the Christian. It is certainly not easy in our sex-saturated society. But it is possible. As Roger Crook explains,

> In spite of what you may read, and in spite of what you may be told, continence is in no sense abnormal and in no sense unhealthy. A rejection of your sexual nature, a denial that you have a sex drive, is abnormal and unhealthy. But a recognition of that drive and a deliberate, rational decision to abstain is both desirable and possible.[4]

To some an aid to continence is masturbation. So taboo has been this subject that up until recent days very little discussion was found about it, even in the most thorough Christian and psychological periodicals. Perhaps we have avoided the subject because we have not known what to say about it.

In the midst of the silence and confusion, two factors seem to be clear. First, there is no actual statement on the matter in the Scriptures. The only experience remotely relating to the idea in the Bible (Gen. 38:1-11) actually relates to the interruption of coitus and not to masturbation. Second, we can affirm that there is no problem with masturbation from a scientific point of view. Any such claim is nothing more than an old wives' tale.

There is a principle that might relate to the matter, and that is the principle of the thought life. This is the principle Jesus introduced in his Sermon on the Mount when he took the actions of murder and adultery beyond the physical act to the psychological motivation for the act. "Every one who looks on a woman to lust for her," said Jesus, "has committed adultery with her already in his heart" (Matt. 5:28). This principle of the thought life is also referred to by Paul in the final chapter of his Philippian letter. So important is our thought life to our Christian life that we should only allow into our minds those things that are true, honorable, right, pure, lovely, and of good repute (Phil. 4:8). Each Christian must apply this biblical principle to his own life to determine where it will lead him.

Tim Stafford clearly categorizes the arguments usually given for and against masturbation.

According to Stafford, some claim masturbation is OK because of the silence of the Scriptures. Since God specifically dealt with every other form of deviant sexual expression, God would have included masturbation if it were wrong for the Christian. The physiological necessity of it because of the regular buildup of semen in males is also cited. Masturbation is the most acceptable method of releasing the pressure. Arguments against it include the conclusion that masturbation is usually associated with lurid fantasies which lead to lust. Others point out that it can become a crutch which causes a person to withdraw from the world and avoid facing his problems.[5] Each individual will have to follow the leadership of the Holy Spirit on this matter.

Perhaps the best aid to continence is sublimation. Here the sexual urge is not stimulated but sublimated into other creative forms of activity. Physical exercise such as jogging or tennis, mental exercise like reading or writing, artistic activity such as painting or sewing, and social activity like involvement in helping other people can provide avenues in which the strong sexual drive can be sublimated and acceptably released.

Such "sexual fasting" is, of course, not easy. In the personal testimony of one who for over forty years faced the problem,

> Relinquishment is not a state at which we arrive suddenly, nor once and for all. It is a slow pilgrimage, and there are many stumblings and bruisings along the way . . . . You meet it in the power of God. All of life is a struggle; if it were not this one, it would be another. You just accept what is yours, offer it up to God, and get on with the business of living.[6]

CONCLUSION

A theme for an evangelistic emphasis several years ago was, "Christ IS the Answer." Placards and posters with this theme were posted all over Atlanta, Georgia. In the Baptist hospital, posters proclaiming "Christ IS the Answer" were on the bulletin boards. Someone passing by had scribbled at the bottom of one of the posters, "If Christ is the answer, what is the question?"

The questions for most singles is, How can I find meaning in my life? and How can I deal with the matter of sex? These were the questions plaguing this single again of yesteryear. She came to Jesus and in him found an answer to her questions. If you will turn to him, you too will discover that he will lead you to a better way, a way of peace and fulfillment.

11
The Satisfied Single: *Paul*
Philippians 4:11; 1 Corinthians 7

There are many portraits which have been painted of the apostle Paul. He is shown as a Hebrew and as a Hellenist. He is discussed as a Pharisee and as a Christian. Some have focused on his message while others have focused on his missionary journeys. He is quoted as an authority on almost every subject, including marriage.

One lady was so tired of her husband quoting Paul to her that she decided the first thing she would do when she got to heaven was to trip the apostle Paul! Let me set another portrait of Paul beside the others. Picture Paul as a satisfied single. "I have learned to be content," Paul said to the Philippian Christians, "in whatever state I am" (Phil. 4:11).

We do not know for certain if Paul were ever married. Some have said that for a person to be a Pharisee he not only had to be married but also had to be a father. The document used to support this idea, however, is from a time later than Paul's day, so we cannot be sure the same conditions existed then.[1] William Barclay refers to another early Jewish document which mentions seven who would be excommunicated from heaven and the list begins, "A Jew who has no wife."[2] We simply do not know for sure.

Whether or not Paul had been married at one time, 1 Corinthians 7 makes it clear that he was single. Either by choice or by circumstance, either because he had never been married or because something happened to his wife, Paul was single when he wrote the Corinthian letter. And he was thoroughly satisfied with his condition. He was not longing to be married. He was happy being single.

To the Corinthians, Paul said that it is possible to be a satisfied single. In fact, in some cases, he felt it was even better than to be married. In verse 1 Paul stated, "It is good for a man not to touch a woman." (Although this may be a quote from their letter, Paul nevertheless supports it as his idea in other places.) In verse 7 he added, "Yet I wish that all men were even as I myself am" (that is, single). In verse 8 he suggested, "But I say to the unmarried and to widows that it is good for them if they remain even as I." In verses 25-26 he said, "Now concerning the [unmarried] . . . . I think then that . . . in view of the present distress, that it is good for a man to remain as he is." In verse 40 he spoke of widows, saying, "But in my opinion she is happier if she remains as she is." Then, the heart of his argument, in verses 32-35 Paul declared,

> But I want you to be free from concern. One who is unmarried is concerned about the things of the Lord, how he may please the Lord; but one who is married is concerned about the things of the world, how he may please his wife, and his interests are divided . . . . And say this I for your own benefit . . . to secure undistracted devotion to the Lord.

What Paul proclaimed was that the single life is OK. It is possible to be single and satisfied. This was a strange proclamation in the day in which Paul lived. The idea of celibacy or singleness was not widely accepted in any culture in Paul's time.

In the Old Testament Jewish world, marriage was almost universal. The main people who were not married were those who through physical damage, either accidental or purposeful, were unable to perform sexually (Deut. 23:1; Lev. 21:20; 22:24). There were no spinsters, and there was not even a word for *bachelor* in the Old Testament.[3]

There were widows, of course, but these were usually removed from widowhood through the practice of levirate marriage where a brother of the deceased husband would marry the widow. If a widow was not claimed by a brother of her dead husband or reclaimed by her family, she often lived in disgrace. It is probable that widows even had to wear special garments to identify themselves as widows.[4]

The same feeling carried over into the New Testament period. The Jews expected everyone to marry. Apparently every member of the Sanhedrin had to be married. Marriage was considered the normal state of life. This basic idea in the Jewish mind was also prevalent in almost every other culture of that day.

Yet it was in that kind of situation that Paul pronounced this radical idea: Being single is OK. You can be single and satisfied. Because marriage will divide your interests, Paul suggested that a person could develop his personhood and his personal devotion to God better as a single than as a married person.

The early church picked up this theme from Paul and many church fathers in the first three centuries either practiced or praised the single life. By AD 300, in the Council of Elvira, a local Spanish council, celibacy was imposed for the first time on the bishops of that area. Gradually celibacy became the imposed pattern for all of the priests and bishops of the church. Singleness came to be exalted as the highest state for a Christian.

A radical reaction to that idea came in the Reformation period. Celibacy was discarded and marriage was exalted once more as the highest state for a Christian. We are still living in the aftermath of the Reformation thinking. We so strongly advocate marriage that we often attach a certain stigma to singleness.

A friend of mine who is a seminary graduate could not get a church to call him as pastor because he was single. There wasn't anything wrong with him. He had simply chosen not to be married. But the feeling of the churches was so strong against his singleness that he finally decided to seek another profession. We often promote the same idea with some of our caustic remarks to those not yet married. To counter that mind-set we need to use the message of 1 Corinthians 7 to affirm the often forgotten alternative of singleness.

This is vital today because more and more people are finding themselves in the single state. Sometimes it is a matter of choice. On other occasions it is a matter of circumstances. According to recent statistics there are nearly fifty million singles in the United States today. One out of every three adults is single. And the young singles segment of our population is growing over five times as fast as the nation as a whole.

To the growing numbers of singles, we need to share the good news that they can be single and satisfied. In Paul's example we see some hints as to how it can happen.

PUT MARRIAGE IN PROPER PERSPECTIVE

First, Paul was a satisfied single because he put marriage in its proper perspective. Simply put, Paul realized that marriage was not for everyone. Singleness was a viable option for the Christian.

A feeling pervades our culture today which pressures individuals into marriage and attributes to singleness a certain stigma. Some people are frantic if they are not married by the time they are out of college. Being twenty-one and not married is a state of despair for many young people.

We need to realize that there is something worse than not being married—being married to the wrong person.

There is a state much more uncomfortable than being out of wedlock—being in wedlock but out of the will of God.

There are, of course, some disadvantages that singles have to face. There is a certain degree of loneliness inherent in single life. The disadvantage of a higher income tax rate is something I do not need to say much about. There is also the fact that much of our society and much of our church life is structured on a family basis and singles are often left out. In addition, there are the married friends who are always trying to play cupid and match you up with somebody who would be "just perfect" for you.

Nevertheless, it is possible to be single and satisfied. That secret is being discovered by many singles today who are not yearning to get married. They are enjoying being single.

Paul knew that some satisfaction as a single because he put marriage in its proper perspective. He saw it as *an* option and not *the* option for the Christian.

REMAINED SINGLE FOR THE PROPER REASONS

Paul was a satisfied single because he remained single for the proper reasons.

One bachelor said that he stayed single because every time he looked at television commercials he learned that women are anemic, have stringy hair with split ends, have large pores, are overweight, and have rough hands. You might agree or disagree with his conclusions, but the point remains that there are good reasons and bad reasons for remaining single.

Consider some of the bad reasons. Some remain single *because of too strong parental attachment.* One couple in Portugal was engaged for thirty-five years until the man's mother died and then they were married.

Some remain single *because of personality quirks.* They may be too shy or bashful to ever take the initiative in developing a relationship. Or they may be afraid of getting too close to another person.

Others remain single *because of self-centeredness* which is probably a good reason. Marriage is a two-way relationship with each partner seeking to meet the other person's needs. Some are so self-centered that they can never become concerned enough about the other person's needs. Whether that kind of person gets married or remains single, he is going to be unhappy.

These are some of the wrong reasons for remaining single, but many choose to be single or remain single for normal and healthy reasons.

Some remain single because of *geography*. That is, they live in areas where they have little opportunity to meet compatible mates. This is something beyond their control.

Some choose to remain single because of *economy*. With equal opportunities for career possibilities beginning to open to women, many opt for a career rather than for marriage.

Others choose to remain single because of *theology*. They feel a divine call to a special work. Phillip Brooks remained single mainly for that reason. One of the great love stories of ancient times is that of Heloise and Abelard, both unusual scholars. Abelard, while serving as her tutor, seduced Heloise and then married her. Immediately after the wedding, she went straight for the convent. Why? Because she felt it would be impossible for Abelard to be Abelard, to fulfill God's task for his life, while married. So she chose singleness for him.[5] Earlier still, a man named Paul chose to be single, as he said in 1 Corinthians 7, so he might be free to do what God wanted him to do.

Paul was a satisfied single for he chose to be single not because of some pathological problem but because it would free him to do God's will for his life. He remained single for the right reason.

DEVELOPED OTHER MEANINGFUL RELATIONSHIPS

There is a third reason Paul was a satisfied single. He developed other meaningful relationships. He substituted comradeship with friends for companionship with a mate.

Inherent in human life is the drive to relate to other people. One psychologist says that the strongest drive in the human heart—stronger than the will to pleasure that Freud mentioned, stronger than the will to power that Adler described, stronger than the will to meaning that Frankl emphasized, is the will to relate.[6] Karl Menninger has said, "The establishment or re-establishment of relationship with fellow human beings is the basic architecture of normal life."[7] It is to satisfy this basic architecture of normal life, this relationship-hunger, that God instituted marriage.

Paul met the need of relationship and discovered an inner satisfaction by developing close friends. If you will study Paul's life, you will discover that he had a genius for friendship. "My co-workers," "my brothers," "I hold you up constantly in my prayers." These were phrases that appeared repeatedly in Paul's letters. A good example is the closing chapter of the letter to the Roman Christians. In that one chapter he mentioned twenty-seven names. He added a special word about most of them, which indicates they were friends and not just a list of names.

Paul discovered that it is possible to satisfy the relationship-hunger of the human heart in meaningful friendships outside of marriage as well as in the unity of marriage, in comradeship, as well as in companionship.

No man is an island. You cannot survive in isolation

from other people. But if you can develop meaningful relationships with friends, then you, like Paul, can be a satisfied single.

PUT HIS LIFE IN GOD'S HANDS

One last thing. Paul was a satisfied single because, as a single, he put his life in the hands of God.

The key to your contentment and satisfaction as a person is not your marital status but whether you have turned your life over to God. That is the primary relationship of life. If you do not have that primary relationship right, whatever else you do does not matter. If you marry but are not in right relationship with God, you will not be satisfied. If you have children but are not in right relationship with God, you will not be satisfied. If you make a lot of money but are not in right relationship with God, you will not be satisfied. If you put marriage in the proper perspective and remain single for the right reasons and develop relationships with friends but are not in right relationship with God, you will not be satisfied.

The key is what you do in your relationship with God. Paul had already taken care of it. Paul had put God in charge of his life. "For to me, to live is Christ" (Phil. 1:21), Paul said. And that in the end is why he could say, "[Married or single,] I have learned to be content in whatever circumstance I am."

12
The Supreme Single: *Jesus*
Luke 2:52

As Leonardo da Vinci was working on the unfinished painting of the Last Supper one morning, a friend watched. Entranced with the two silver cups in the picture in front of Jesus on the table, he mentioned the splendor of their design. Taking his brush, da Vinci immediately blotted them both out. "It is not those cups I want you to see," he exclaimed. "It is that face—the face of Christ!"[1]

In our look at the singles of the Bible we too must focus our attention on Jesus. These other singles can provide helpful insights, but for the Christian Jesus' life must be our focus point. He is the supreme single in whose life the Christian single of today will find his ultimate example. "For you have been called for this purpose," the Bible says, "since Christ also suffered for you, leaving you an example for you to follow in his Steps" (1 Pet. 2:21). Jesus is our single example.

There have been attempts to deny the singleness of Jesus. William A. Phipps suggested that possibility in a journal article several years ago.[2] This article was followed by a book entitled, *Was Jesus Married?*[3] In the book, Phipps analyzed the question thoroughly in the context of the sexual attitudes prevalent in ancient Judaism and the silence of the New Testament on the matter. He concluded:

Was Jesus married? The New Testament assumes that Jesus had normal sexuality and sexual desire, both of which are

> essential for humanness and prerequisites to marriage. Those bio-social qualities were indicated in the following ways: Jesus' male foreskin was cut; his general and individual relationships to the opposite sex display no sexual phobias; and his maturity was gained through exposure to the inevitable temptations of manhood. Jesus unreservedly approved conviviality and connubiality and did not suggest that either was defiling per se. In view of no overt evidence to the contrary, it is reasonable that the silence of the New Testament should be interpreted to mean that Jesus internalized the Jewish mores pertaining to sex and marriage.[4]

That is, that Jesus was married and participated in sex. He added a statement which perhaps was his motivation for the entire study: "If such an opinion becomes widely endorsed it should have a beneficial effect on the Christian church and on the quality of life that western man idealizes as truly human."[5]

Phipps used the silence of the New Testament as a platform from which to leap from his assumptions to his conclusions. However, the facts that Jesus could have participated in marriage, that Jesus had natural sexual desires, and that Jesus approved of marriage do not by any means lead us, by necessity, to the conclusion that Jesus was, therefore, married. Phipps' arguments are clever at times but not at all convincing.

That Jesus had a mother and father is clearly stated in the Scriptures, and reference is made to Jesus' brothers and sisters as well. Would so significant a person in his life as a wife not have been introduced to us? I think not. The silence of the New Testament on the matter lends more support to the claim that Jesus was single than to the claim that Jesus was married.

Was Jesus ever married? No. He chose singleness not because celibacy was necessary, not because sex was nasty, but in order to allow him the freedom to fulfill God's purpose in his life. As our example, he does not dictate the necessity of singleness for us, but his example does affirm the viability of singleness if we so chose.

In Matthew's Gospel Jesus suggested three reasons a person might choose to remain single. "For there are different reasons why men cannot marry," Jesus said. "Some because they were born that way; others because men made them that way; and others do not marry for the sake of the Kingdom of heaven" (Matt. 19:12, TEV).

Physiological reasons may lead a person to remain single. Jesus probably had in mind those who were born with congenital problems which would make marriage difficult or impossible. The principle can be extended to include those who because of their emotional or mental temperament are just not interested in marriage.

Sociological reasons may also lead a person to remain single. The reference of Jesus is probably to the practice of mutilation which was a common practice in the ancient world to render slaves incapable of marital intimacy. The principle can be extended to include those who because of societal reason choose not to be married. "Unhappy childhood homes, ill treatment of children by family members or others, lack of education, influence of the news media, and general societal changes—all these have conditioned many persons against the prospect of marriage."[6]

There are also *spiritual reasons* that lead a person to remain single. A person may choose to remain single in order to fulfill the ministry to which God has called him. At times the choice may be conscious and deliberate. Faced by a decision between marrying a specific individual or giving oneself unhindered to the task before you, the latter option is selected. On other occasions, it is an unconscious choice. A person commits himself to a task. The weeks and months pass with the person absorbed in what he is doing. He does not choose to be single, but his absorption in the task prevents him from deliberately choosing a mate.

Whichever reason has led you to be a single—physiological, sociological, or spiritual—the fact remains that Jesus is the supreme example of how that singleness is to be lived out. Let's see what we can learn from his example.

THE PRODUCTIVITY

At the age of twelve, in the Temple, Jesus confronted his parents with a perplexing query, "Wist ye not that I must be about my Father's business?" (Luke 2:49, KJV). On the cross, as the painful anguish rushed to a conclusion, Jesus pierced the air with a triumphant proclamation, "It is finished" (John 19:30). Between those two brackets was a life so productive that it could be said of him,

> Nineteen centuries have come and gone, and today He is the central figure of the human race and the leader of the column of progress. I am far within the mark when I say that all the armies that ever marched, and all the navies that ever sailed, and all the parliaments that ever sat, and all the kings that ever reigned, put together, have not affected the life of man upon this earth as has that one solitary life.[7]

What a productive life Jesus had. Judged by his contemporaries to be a failure, whose life ended in a Roman crucifixion, he has been proved to be history's greatest success.

Two misconceptions about Jesus' success often prevent us from experiencing the full impact of his example.

One misconception has to do with the nature of Jesus' productivity. "He might have been a single," we protest, "but he was also the Son of God. I can't match his life. I can't be a success like him."

What was the measure of his success? Look again at his

cry from the cross. Our English versions translate his cry
to be, "It is finished" (John 19:30). In the Greek it is only
one word, *tetelestai*. This word means "a thing matured"
or "a task brought to perfection." The same idea appeared when Jesus told his disciples that he had finished
the work that God gave him to do (John 17:4). He realized
his potential. That was the measure of his success.

Granted, as the Son of God, his potential was greater
than ours. His productivity was beyond ours because his
potential was beyond ours. We cannot match his productivity. We can, however, follow his pattern.

For Jesus, the pattern of success was to finish the work
that God had given him to do, to match his practice to his
potential. This is the thrust of Robert Raines' definition of
success.

> Success means the integration of myself. What I mean by
> that is a congruence of my inside and my outside so that my
> outside relationships and roles fully, clearly, and authen-
> tically express what is real and what is really going on in my
> inside, so that the inner and outer person are in focus.[8]

A management motivator told a group that success was
when an individual reached the maximum potential available to him at any given moment. That is the pattern of
success in Jesus' life.

Confucius is purported to have said, "Success is relative. The more success you have, the more relatives!" He's
right. Success is relative. It is relative to your potential.

To see Jesus as a single example is not to say, "I want to
match his productivity," but to declare, "I want to follow
his pattern." That means to realize our God given potential and to finish the work that God has given us to do.

Where do you begin? Begin with an honest inventory of
your life. To accept yourself is the first step toward success.

Honesty will lead to a recognition of our limitations, as well as our potential, so that we can chart our life within those two brackets. To aim too low is as much a road to failure as to aim too high.

To end your life with the cry of victory, *tetelestai,* does not mean that you have to accomplish what Jesus did. It means that, like Jesus, you will finish the work God has given you to do, invest the gifts God has given you to use, and live as the child of God he has made you to be.

THE PROBLEMS

Another misconception of Jesus' productivity has to do with the pathway that leads to success. "Sure Jesus finished the work that God gave him to do," we agree. "But look at all he had going for him."

Let's approach it from the other direction. Consider, for a moment, what he had going against him. That he was a "man of sorrows, and acquainted with grief" (Isa. 53:3) is not so much a definition of his character as it is a description of his circumstances. From every direction, Jesus knew the reality of rejection.

He was rejected first of all *by his family.* His family did not so much offer opposition as skepticism and concern. On one occasion his brothers taunted him to go to Jerusalem and prove he was the Messiah. They did not really expect him to do it, however, for the Bible says, "For not even His brothers were believing in Him" (John 7:5). On another occasion his family tried to take him home for his own safety. "And when His own people heard of this, they went out to take custody of Him; for they were saying, 'He has lost His senses' " (Mark 3:21).

Jesus was also rejected *by his friends.* On a return trip to Nazareth, his hometown, Jesus went to the synagogue to teach. The people were astonished initially. Soon their astonishment changed to offense. "Is not this the carpenter's son?'' they asked. "Is not His mother called Mary, and His brothers, James and Joseph and Simon and Judas? And His sisters, are they not all with us? Where then did this man get all of these things?'' The Gospel writer concluded, "And He did not do many miracles there because of their unbelief'' (Matt. 13:55-58).

The religious leaders of the day rejected Jesus as well. They saw Jesus as a rabble-rouser and imposter. Instead of recognizing him for who he was, they labeled him "a gluttonous man and a drunkard, a friend of tax-gatherers and sinners'' (Matt. 11:19). Their opposition was crystalized when he raised Lazarus from the dead. "So from that day on,'' the Bible says, "they planned together to kill Him'' (John 11:53).

Even *his disciples* rejected him. Judas, one of the twelve, participated in the plot that led to the arrest of Jesus (John 18:2-3). In Jesus' moment of deepest anguish in the garden of Gethsemane, the three disciples closest to him fell asleep (Matt. 26:40-45). Peter, who so boldly proclaimed his faith, denied Jesus three times, even cursing his name (John 18:15-27). When the crisis came and the soldiers arrested Jesus, the disciples fled (Matt. 26:56).

If you think Jesus had everything going his way, you are mistaken. "He came to His own, and those who were His own did not receive Him'' (John 1:11). That is the true picture. Rejected by his friends, opposed by his enemies, executed by his government—those were the predominant factors in his life.

Jesus' productivity came, then, not because of pleasant circumstances but in spite of unpleasant ones. Instead of allowing his circumstances to make him bitter, Jesus used them to make himself better. Instead of stumbling blocks, his obstacles became the stepping-stones to the fulfillment of God's purpose in his life.

How often we are thwarted by circumstantial failure.

"Bad circumstances" is the excuse we hang our failure on. But everybody has circumstances.

You say it is hard to become involved in God's work as a single. Do you think it is any easier when you have a wife and children to whom you must devote time and attention?

You say it is difficult to give your money to God's work as a single because you don't have enough money. Do you think there is any more money when your resources have to cover the expenses of a growing family?

Everybody has circumstances! The key to Jesus' success was that he used his circumstances instead of letting his circumstances use him.

"To a brave man, good luck and bad luck are his right and left hand. He uses both." That suggestion, made by Catherine of Siena many centuries ago, is a beautiful description of Jesus and a bountiful prescription for us.

In a sermon entitled "Gratitude and Coping," John Claypool gives an example of how Jesus faced his problems and found productivity in spite of them. The story Claypool uses is found in Mark 6:30-44. A multitude of people followed Jesus to hear him teach. When dinner time arrived, he was surrounded by thousands of hungry people who needed to be fed. That was a seemingly overwhelming problem. Read the story again and you will discover the three steps Jesus took. First, he faced the problem. He rejected the strategy of escapism. Second, he identified the resources that were inherent in the situation. Third, he took the resources that were available, thanked God for them, and then went about the task of meeting the hunger of the crowd. The hinge on which the whole process turned was that Jesus began to do the best he could with what he had.[9]

Despite the problems that perpetually plagued him,

Jesus matched his practice with his potential. That was the measure of his success.

THE PATTERN

How can you as a single duplicate the productiveness of Jesus' life? How can you share in his single blessings? The pattern is found in the paradigm Jesus gave for discipleship. This paradigm, of course, relates to all of Jesus' followers, married or single.

The paradigm was given by Jesus in response to a question. "Teacher, which is the great commandment in the Law?" someone asked. Jesus responded, " 'YOU SHALL LOVE THE LORD YOUR GOD WITH ALL YOUR HEART, AND WITH ALL YOUR SOUL, AND WITH ALL YOUR MIND.' This is the great and foremost commandment. And a second is like it, 'YOU SHALL LOVE YOUR NEIGHBOR AS YOURSELF' " (Matt. 22:37-38). As disciples of Jesus, we are to obey his commandments. And this is the greatest commandment, the commandment to love.

Notice first the necessity of *self-love.* "Love your neighbor *as [you love] yourself,"* Jesus said. The first obligation for any person who wishes to make a significant contribution to the world is to take proper care of himself.

This means physical care. Modern medicine has developed methods for heart transplants, eye transplants, and kidney transplants. But have you ever heard of a body transplant? No. There is no such possibility. The body you have is the only one you will ever have. Therefore, you need to take care of it.

Some problems of health, of course, are beyond our control. However, the problems which come because of failure to follow good health practices, diet deficiencies, and lack of exercise are responsibilities that we Christians can do something about.

Paul Tournier has suggested, "Most illnesses do not, as is generally thought, come like a bolt out of the blue. The ground is prepared for years, through faulty diet, intemperance, overwork, and moral conflicts, slowly eroding the subject's vitality."[10] Much of our physical debilitation is caused by unhealthy living habits.

Does this mean you should become a jogger? Not necessarily. One man said that every time the desire to jog arises in him, he stays real still for a few minutes, and the desire passes. I can identify with that. Jogging is not for everyone. Try walking or a bicycle or tennis or racquet ball or any other form of recreation. The point is that in our day, when the only exercise most people get is jumping to conclusions, running down friends, sidestepping responsibility, and pushing their luck, we need to become concerned about the proper exercise that leads to a healthy body.

Does this mean you should become a health food nut? Not necessarily. Not everyone can survive on artichoke bread, sunflower seeds, alfalfa sprouts, and raw honey. The point is that in our day when most of us tend toward becoming junk food junkies, we need to give careful attention to our diet.

Our body is the only one that we will ever have. We need to take care of it. That's how love for self will manifest itself.

Love for self will also lead us to mental care. Ours is a day of reawakened concern for our physical well-being. A recent Gallup poll indicated that 47 percent of all Americans now claim to participate in some sort of exercise. Even the United States Dairy Association is getting into the act. They have developed a jogging program for their dairy cows to firm up their flabby muscles and build up their hearts. (And we thought cows were contented!)

In our day of infatuation with good health, we continue

to neglect one part of our bodies—our minds. If it is true, as one man has suggested, that only 5 percent of the people in our world think, 10 percent think they think, and 85 percent would rather die than think, then mental hygiene is one of the most neglected disciplines today.

A good mental hygiene program is outlined in Philippians 4:8. Think on the right things. That is the admonition of Paul. Cultivate your mind by thinking on truth as opposed to falsehood, on the serious as opposed to the frivolous, on the right as opposed to the convenient, on the clean as opposed to the dirty, on the loving as opposed to the discordant, on the positive as opposed to the negative.

Love for self means that you want to become all that God made you to be. How does that happen? Don't start with your character. Don't start with your habits. Don't start with your actions. Start with your thought life, for what you are is determined by what you think. Develop your mind.

Love for self will also lead us to spiritual care. To develop our body and mind is not enough. More important is the development of our spiritual nature. How much time do you spend in "soul culture"?

Charlie Shedd suggested five habits that will lead to spiritual development: (1) pray diligently; (2) worship regularly; (3) pray daily; (4) give systematically; and (5) serve faithfully.[11]

Facing life as a Christian single begins with a healthy concern for self which leads to physical, mental, and spiritual growth. A single often will have to concentrate almost exclusively on this dimension for a time before being ready to move into the other dimensions of Jesus' paradigm.

In Jesus' paradigm we also see the need for *other-love*. Label self-love as concern. Other-love can be called compassion. Our love for others, according to Jesus, is the sign by which people will know that we are truly his disciples (John 13:35).

Did you see the "Peanuts" cartoon strip in which Lucy gave Linus a lesson on human nature? She drew a heart on the wall with a crayon, coloring half of it red and leaving the other half plain. "This," she said to Linus, "is a picture of the human heart. One side is filled with love and the other side is filled with hate. These two forces are constantly at war with each other." In the last picture Linus clutched his chest and said, "I think I understand what you mean. I can feel them fighting."[12]

On more than one occasion we too have felt the conflicting emotions of hate and love struggling on the inside. Jesus was aware of this conflict himself, for no other person was so plagued by bitter, undeserved hatred than was Jesus. Yet, time and time again Jesus repeated that equal in importance to loving God is loving your neighbor, even your enemy, as you love yourself.

How can we do that? A giant step in our understanding will come when we realize that this love for others is not a "feeling kind" of love but an "acting kind" of love. Jesus' example is helpful here. We don't always know how Jesus felt. Instead, we see his love in the things he did.

Jesus approached a man covered with rags (Mark 1:40-45). The stench almost knocked Jesus over. The feelings of repulsion probably began to arise in Jesus. Love didn't change his feeling, but it changed his actions. Jesus reached out and touched the man. Love is something you do.

In the story of the good Samaritan, the hero is the one who stopped to help a man who had been beaten (Luke 10:25-37). Because of the bitter hatred between Jews and Samaritans, I am sure that this Samaritan had bad feelings toward the beaten Jew. Yet, the Samaritan treated the man's hurt, took care of his needs, and provided the injured man with assistance. It was not a matter of feeling. It was a matter of action. Love is something you do.

Or look at Jesus himself. If you want to know how he felt about the world, see him weeping over a city that would not repent. If you want to know how he felt about the ordeal before him, see him in Gethsemane where he sweat drops of blood. If you want to know how he felt about dying for the sins of the world, look at him as he staggered up the rugged trail to Golgotha. See his dry, parched lips longing for some liquid. Gaze at the agonizing pain that was revealed in the drawn lines of his face. Hear him as he cried out, "MY GOD, MY GOD, WHY HAST THOU FORSAKEN ME?" (Matt. 27:46). That's how he felt. But if you want to see his love, look at the cross where despite his feelings, despite the hostility, despite the shame, he died a painful death for a sinful world and you will see very clearly that love is something you do.

Christian love is not based on feeling. It is based on action. When Jesus said to love your neighbor as you love yourself, he did not mean to feel toward him in a certain way. He was not urging you to conjure up some special feeling within. He was simply saying that, whatever the feelings that erupt from within, act toward all men with love, treating them the way you want them to treat you.

There is a third dimension in Jesus' paradigm which is *God-love.* Label this commitment. Not only does the Bible repeatedly admonish us to love God but it also illustrates how such a love will manifest itself in our lives.

The Bible says to love God means to hate evil (Ps. 97:10). Do you? Do you refuse to expose yourself to the filth of the world and oppose it with all that is within you?

The Bible says to love God means to keep his commandments (Ex. 20:6; Deut. 11:1). Do you? Are you obedient to God's will? Do you do the things he wants you to do?

The Bible says to love God means to serve him (Deut. 10:12). Do you? Is your purpose in life to bear fruit for him and thus to glorify him before the world?

Our love for God is reflected not just by our professions. Words are cheap. Our love is reflected by a consistent commitment in our lives to oppose evil, obey God's commandments, and serve him.

"Dear Lord, Thy will be done. Nothing more. Nothing less. Nothing else. Amen." That prayer is a model for every Christian.

Concern, compassion, commitment—these are all elements of the love that should characterize the life of a Christian single.

CONCLUSION

Teilhard de Chardin, French paleontologist and theologian, once said, "Someday, after mastering the winds, waves, tides, and gravity we shall harness—for God—the energies of love. And then, for the second time in the history of the world, man will discover fire."[13]

By harnessing the energy of love and releasing it in the actions of our lives, we can set our communities and our world ablaze with the glory of God.

Notes

Chapter One

1. S. I. McMillen, *None of These Diseases* (Westwood, N.J.: Fleming H. Revell, 1963), pp. 71-73.

2. Alice Kosner, "Starting Over: What Divorced Women Discover," *McCalls* (March, 1979), p. 160.

3. James E. Kilgore, "Dealing with Initial Isolation and Loneliness at the End of Marriage," John G. Cull and Richard E. Hardy, eds., *Deciding on Divorce: Personal and Family Considerations* (Springfield, Ill.: Charles C. Thomas, 1974), p. 34.

4. Sarah Jepson, *For the Love of Singles* (Carol Stream, Ill.: Creation House, Inc., 1970), p. 63.

5. Kosner, p. 22.

6. Edith Deen, *All of the Women of the Bible* (New York: Harper and Brothers, 1955), p. 266.

Chapter Two

1. James C. Hefley, *A Dictionary of Illustrations* (Grand Rapids, Mich.: Zondervan Publishing House, 1971), p. 311.

2. Linda Bird Francke, "Going It Alone," *Newsweek* (September 4, 1978), p. 76.

3. Ibid.

4. "In the Professions, Women Are Moving Up," *U. S. News and World Report* (September 4, 1978), p. 59.

5. Cleveland McDonald, *Creating A Successful Christian Marriage* (Grand Rapids, Mich.: Baker Book House, 1975), p. 314.

6. Kosner, p. 22.

7. Peter Stein, *Single* (Englewood Cliffs, N.J.: Prentice-Hall, Inc., 1976), p. 26.

8. Ibid.

9. Jack Horn, "Solved: The Mystery of the Hawthorne Effect," *Psychology Today* (December, 1976), p. 40.

10. James P. Wesberry, *Meditations for Happy Christians* (Nashville, Tn.: Broadman Press, 1973), p. 50.

Chapter Three

1. James Randolph Hobbs, *The Pastor's Manual* (Nashville, Tn.: Broadman Press, 1934), p. 165.

2. *Quote,* Vol. 77, p.3.

3. John W. Drakeford, *Wisdom for Today's Family* (Nashville, Tn.: Broadman Press, 1978), p. 66.

4. David R. Mace, *Whom God Hath Joined* (Philadelphia, Pa.: The Westminster Press, 1973), p. 67.

5. Herbert J. Miles, *The Dating Game* (Grand Rapids, Mich.: Zondervan Publishing House, 1975), pp. 58-59.

6. Ibid., p. 46.

7. Albert I. Gordon, *Intermarriage: Interfaith, Interracial, Interethnic* (Boston, Mass.: Beacon Press, 1964), p. 372.

8. *The Pensacola News-Journal,* September 2, 1979, p. 1c.

9. Jack R. Taylor, *One Home Under God* (Nashville, Tn.: Broadman Press, 1974), p. 74.

Chapter Four

1. Eugenia Price, *The Unique World of Woman* (Grand Rapids, Mich.: Zondervan Publishing House, 1969), p. 38.

2. Quoted in Gary R. Collins, *Overcoming Anxiety* (Santa Anna, Ca.: Vision House Publishers, 1973), p. 146.

3. Leighton Ford, *New Man, New World* (Waco, Tx.: Word Books, 1972), p. 28.

4. *Standard College Dictionary* (New York: Funk & Wagnalls, 1977), p. 287.

5. Gail Sheehy, *Passages* (New York: E. P. Dutton & Co., Inc., 1974), p. 45.

6. *Standard College Dictionary,* p. 881.

7. Donald E. Demaray, *Pulpit Giants* (Chicago, Ill.: Moody Press, 1973), p. 55.

8. John W. Drakeford, *The Great Sex Swindle* (Nashville, Tn.: Broadman Press, 1966), p. 55.

9. Jill Morgan, *A Man of the Word* (Grand Rapids, Mich.: Baker Book House, 1972), p. 23.

Chapter Five

1. Harry N. Hollis, Jr., et. al, *Christian Freedom for Women** (Nashville, Tn.: Broadman Press, 1975), p. 22.

2. Letha Scanzoni and Nancy Hardesty, *All We're Meant to Be* (Waco, Tx.: Word Books, 1974), p. 204.

3. Eugenia Price, *God Speaks to Women Today* (Grand Rapids, Mich.: Zondervan Publishing House, 1964), p. 89.

4. C. Welton Gaddy, *Profile of a Christian Citizen* (Nashville, Tn.: Broadman Press, 1974), p. 17.

5. Marilyn McGinnis, *Single* (Old Tappan, N. J.: Fleming H. Revell, 1974), p. 38.

6. Price, *God Speaks to Women Today,* p. 91.

Chapter Six

1. For a treatment of the relationship between Ruth and Boaz see my book, *Famous Couples of the Bible* (Nashville, Tn.: Broadman Press, 1979), pp. 70-80.

2. Liston O. Mills, ed., *Perspectives on Death* (Nashville, Tn.: Abingdon Press, 1969), p. 173.

3. Ibid., p. 169.

4. Vance Havner, *Though I Walk Through the Valley* (Old Tappan, N. J.: Fleming H. Revell, 1974), p. 91.

5. C. S. Lewis, *A Grief Observed* (New York: The Seabury Press, 1963), p. 13.

6. Myron C. Madden, *Raise the Dead* (Waco, Tx.: Word Books, 1976), p. 35.

7. Mills, p. 266.

8. Phyllis Martin, "Widow," *Good Housekeeping* (March, 1976), p. 18.

Chapter Seven

1. *Quote,* Vol. 76, p. 363.

2. A. D. Dennison, *Give It to Me Straight, Doctor* (Grand Rapids, Mich.: Zondervan Publishing House, 1972), p. 76.

3. James E. McReynolds, *America's No. 1 Drug Problem* (Nashville, Tn.: Broadman Press, 1977), pp. 49-50.

4. Cecil Osborne, *The Art of Understanding Your Mate* (Grand Rapids, Mich.: Zondervan Publishing House, 1970), p. 113.

5. Drakeford, *Wisdom for Today's Family,* p. 149.

6. Howard J. Clinebell and Charlotte H. Clinebell, *The Intimate Marriage* (New York: Harper & Row, 1970), p. 148.

7. *Dallas Morning News,* July 27, 1978, p. 6c.

8. Bernard Havnik, *Risk & Chance in Marriage* (Waco, Tx.: Word Books, 1972), p. 17.

9. Susan Nelson, "How Battered Women Can Get Help," *Reader's Digest* (May, 1977), p. 83.

10. R. Lofton Hudson, *Till Divorce Do Us Part* (Nashville, Tn.: Thomas Nelson, 1974), p. 83.

Chapter Eight

1. E. Stanley Jones, *Christian Maturity* (New York: Abingdon Press, 1957), p. 351.

2. Britton Wood, *Single Adults Want to Be the Church, Too* (Nashville, Tn.: Broadman Press, 1977).

3. Linda Lawson, *Life As a Single Adult* (Nashville, Tn.: Convention Press, 1975), p. 5.

Chapter Nine

1. George A. Turner and Julius R. Mantey, *The Gospel According to John* (Grand Rapids, Mich.: William B. Eerdmans Publishing Co., n. d.), p. 60.

2. Owen Cooper, *The Future Is Before Us* (Nashville, Tn.: Broadman Press, 1973), pp. 85-86.

3. Gaddy, p. 24.

Chapter Ten

1. Kenneth Chafin, *Is There a Family in the House?* (Waco, Tx.: Word Books, 1978), p. 129.

2. Ibid., pp. 131-132.

3. Margaret Clarkson, *So You're Single!* (Wheaton, Ill.: Harold Shaw Publishers, 1978), p. 79.

4. Roger H. Crook, *An Open Book to the Christian Divorcee* (Nashville, Tn.: Broadman Press, 1974), p. 87.

5. Tim Stafford, *A Love Story* (Grand Rapids, Mich.: Zondervan Publishing House, 1977), pp. 77-83.

6. Clarkson, pp. 81-82.

Chapter Eleven

1. Richard N. Longenecker, *Paul, Apostle of Liberty* (Grand Rapids, Mich.: Baker Book House, 1964), p. 237.

2. William Barclay, *The Letter to the Corinthians,* Revised (Philadelphia, Pa.: The Westminster Press, 1975), p. 68.

3. Hudson, p. 48.

4. O. J. Baab, "Widow," in George A. Buttrick, ed., *The*

Interpreter's Dictionary of the Bible, Vol. IV (Nashville, Tn.: Abingdon Press, 1962), p. 842.

5. William Barclay, *A Spiritual Autobiography* (Grand Rapids, Mich.: William B. Eerdmans Publishing Co., 1975), p. 66.

6. Clinebell and Clinebell, p. 13.

7. Ibid.

Chapter Twelve

1. Richard Hogue, *The Jesus Touch* (Nashville, Tn.: Broadman Press, 1972), pp. 29-30.

2. William A. Phipps, "Did Jesus or Paul Marry?" *Journal of Ecumenical Studies 5* (1968), pp. 741-744.

3. William A. Phipps, *Was Jesus Married* (New York: Harper & Row, 1970).

4. Ibid., p. 69.

5. Ibid., p. 14.

6. Mark Lee, "The Church and the Unmarried," in Gary Collins, ed., *It's OK to Be Single* (Waco, Tx.: Word Books, 1976), p. 47.

7. This is an anonymous essay that can be found in various sources.

8. Robert A. Raines, *Success Is a Moving Target* (Waco, Tx.: Word Books, 1975), p. 35.

9. John Claypool, Sermon delivered at Northminster Baptist Church, Jackson, Mississippi, November 20, 1977.

10. Quoted in Nelson L. Price, *Shadows We Run From* (Nashville, Tn.: Broadman Press, 1975), p. 89.

11. Charlie W. Shedd, *How to Develop a Praying Church* (Nashville, Tn.: Abingdon Press, 1961), p. 29.

12. Robert L. Short, *The Gospel According to Peanuts* (Richmond, Va.: John Knox Press, 1965), pp. 39-40.

13. Quoted in Charles L. Wallis, ed., *The Minister's Manual: 1976 Edition* (New York: Harper & Row, 1976), p. 130.

CONTENTS

WE'RE GOING TO BE RUNNING TRAINING FOR NEW EMPLOYEES AT BART AGAIN THIS YEAR.

I'VE GOT SOME NEWS TO SHARE.

A RETREAT?

OUCH

AND THEY'VE DECIDED TO DO A FIVE-DAY, FOUR-NIGHT RETREAT AT THE END OF THE MONTH.

CHIBA-KUN HAS BEEN PUTTING TOGETHER A PROPOSAL FOR THE PROGRAM

THEY DESIGNED VIRTUAL STORES, DID SOME ROLEPLAYING ACTIVITIES

AND WERE PUT IN GROUPS TO SOLVE PUZZLES AND MAKE MOCK MARKETING VIDEOS.

BART IS IN THE RETAIL BUSINESS. A FRIEND OF MINE NAMED TAKAHASHI-KUN HANDLES HR THERE.

THE POINT OF THE RETREAT IS TO GET THEM WORKING TOGETHER IN CLOSE QUARTERS TO SOLVE PROBLEMS.

WE DID TRAINING FOR THEIR NEW EMPLOYEES LAST YEAR, TOO.

WELL, IF THE RETREAT'S FAR AWAY, NOT AS MANY CAN ATTEND, AND THINGS START TO GET EXPENSIVE.

WHAT'S CHIBA-SAN SO UPSET ABOUT?

JUST THINK HOW NICE IT WILL BE TO DO MORNING EXERCISES AGAINST THE BACKDROP OF MT. FUJI!

OH, COME ON!!!

EEK!

OH, AND SAI-SAN? YOU'LL BE HERE HOLDING DOWN THE FORT FOR THIS ONE.

CHIBA-KUN...

WHAT-EVER. NO TIME TO ARGUE, SO LET'S GET TO WORK.

BUT SAI-SAN LIKES TO TRAVEL, SO HE'S ALWAYS PICKING FAR-OFF PLACES.

EVEN MORE SO IF THE TRAINEES ARE BUSY WITH WORK.

HOW MANY TIMES HAVE WE TOLD YOU TO TALK THE LOCATION OVER WITH US BEFORE DECIDING?!

WAAAH! I'M SO SORRY!

HAAAH...

LIKE HE SAID, WE'LL BE RUNNING A TRAINING RETREAT.

WE CAN'T AFFORD TO SEND UNNECESSARY CREW MEMBERS OUT THAT FAR.

WHAT?!!!

ESSENTIAL STAFF ONLY. THE BEST OF THE BEST.

ALRIGHT. HUDDLE UP, GUYS.

WHYYYYY?!

HE'S ACTING LIKE HE DOESN'T MIND

BUT I KNOW HE WAS REALLY LOOKING FORWARD TO OUR TRIP

SAGAWA-KUN?

"GOT IT. DON'T WORRY ABOUT ME. JUST DO YOUR BEST AT THE RETREAT."

HAAAH.

I REALLY LET KOHEI DOWN THIS TIME.

HEY! SNAP, SNAP!!

HUH?

WATCH OUT FOR WHAT?

QUIT DAWDLING, YOU TWO!

YOU BETTER WATCH OUT.

OOH, SO SHE'S STILL A STUDENT.

WAIT. WHY AM I ANSWERING HIM?!!

DRAAAIN!

ONCE THEY GRADUATE AND FIND JOBS, THEY FALL OUT OF SYNC.

EVEN COUPLES WHO GOT ALONG JUST FINE IN COLLEGE

THINK ABOUT IT. ONCE YOU START WORKING, LIFE GETS A LOT LESS FLEXIBLE.

—SEE YOU INSIDE!

ANYWAY, BUCK UP. DON'T WORRY ABOUT IT TOO MUCH.

OF

SOMETIMES IT GETS SO BAD THEY HAVE TO BREAK UP.

TENSE

i hear
the
sunspot
limit

i hear the sunspot
limit

RUSTLE!

HEARD YOU GOT CHEWED OUT.

TENDOU-SAN...

I KNOW HE COMES ACROSS A BIT HARSH, BUT IT'S NOT BECAUSE HE DISLIKES YOU.

DON'T TAKE IT TOO HARD.

I CAN SEE THAT HE'S RIGHT.

HE MIGHT EVEN BE RIGHT THAT I'M TOO SOFT.

BUT

IT'S NOT

THE FACT THAT HE GOT ANGRY.

WHEN I SAW HER...

UENO-SAN, BACK THERE...

SHE LOOKED LIKE SHE WAS READY TO CRY.

SAGAWA-KUN

DO YOU KNOW WHICH DISABILITY IS MOST ASSOCIATED WITH QUITTING WORK?

QUITE PERCEPTIVE, THIS ONE.

HE'S

HUH?

THE ANSWER'S DEAFNESS.

A LITTLE MIS-UNDERSTANDING ON THE JOB CAN QUICKLY SPIRAL OUT OF CONTROL. AND NEW HIRES ESPECIALLY

HAVE TO JUGGLE RELATIONSHIPS WITH ESTABLISHED COWORKERS. IT'S NO WONDER THEY TIRE OUT.

JUST GOES TO SHOW HOW IMPORTANT COMMUNICATION IS TO THE WORKPLACE.

HONESTLY. A DEAF YOUNGER BROTHER?

AND POOR SAGAWA-KUN GETTING JERKED AROUND LIKE THAT.

WELL, THE REAL REASON I'M WORKING HERE IS THAT THEY LET ME FREELANCE ON THE SIDE.

BUT I COULDN'T TELL HIM THAT. GOTTA KEEP HIS DREAMS ALIVE.

SO WHY'D YOU LIE TO HIM?!

YOU'RE UNBELIEV-ABLE.

あはは
AHAHA

THAT'S CHIBA-KUN'S SITUATION!

RATTLE
ガタ

RATTLE
ガタ

VRRRRM

RATTLE
ガタ

I WAS JUST DOING WHAT I WANTED TO DO.

AND...

VROOM!

IT'S NOT LIKE ONE WAY IS RIGHT AND THE OTHER WRONG.

YOU DON'T HAVE TO APOLOGIZE.

SHE GETS TO DECIDE FOR HERSELF.

SO IF UENO WANTED AN INTERPRETER TO SIGN FOR HER, WE WERE READY TO PROVIDE ONE.

RUMBLE

RUMBLE

I'D LEARNED WHAT TO EXPECT FROM PREVIOUS YEARS, AND IT WAS YOUR FIRST TIME.

THAT'S ALL IT BOILS DOWN TO.

IT'S NOT LIKE YOU DID ANYTHING WRONG.

VSSSHHH

I GUESS WHAT I SAID WAS PRETTY ONE-SIDED. SHOULD'VE EXPLAINED BETTER.

SO

UH...

UM...

AND I REALLY DON'T SEE ANYTHING UNUSUAL.

I'VE LOOKED OVER THE RESULTS OF YOUR TEST

32
耳鼻咽喉科
OTOLARYNGOLOGY

AND YOU SAID NO DIZZINESS OR RINGING IN THE EARS. I'D CHALK IT UP

TO TEMPORARY LOSS DUE TO FATIGUE OR STRESS.

HAVE YOU EXPERIENCED THE SAME SYMPTOM AGAIN SINCE THEN?

YOU SAID YOU WERE BRIEFLY UNABLE TO HEAR AT ALL.

NOTHING TO WORRY ABOUT AT PRESENT.

YES. I HAVE.

OH. I SEE.

IF WE CAN GET SOME DEGREE OF HEARING BACK FOR YOU, IT MIGHT EASE YOUR CONCERNS.
WHY DON'T YOU THINK IT OVER?
MAYA
HELLO! SORRY TO BUG YOU OVER THE WEEKEND. ARE YOU BUSY TODAY? IF YOU HAVE SOME TIME, WOULD YOU LIKE TO COME WITH ME SOMEWHERE?
BZZZZ!
BZZZZ!
OH!
THERE YOU ARE!
SUGIHARA-SENPAI!

LET'S GO, MAYA.

H-HE LOOKS KINDA UPSET.

S-SUGIHARA-SENPAI?

?!

SLUMP

SURPRISE

MOPE

MOPE

MURMUR

YEAH. YEAH. GOT IT. SOUNDS GREAT.

...

WE'LL BE RIGHT THERE!

OH, REALLY? OKAY, GET THINGS STARTED.

MURMUR

MURMUR

WHAT'S UP, YASU?

THIS THING WE'RE GOING TO. DON'T TELL ME IT'S A DATING PARTY.

ALRIGHT. THANKS AGAIN.

...HEY, YOKO.

JUST FORGET IT! LET'S GO!

WHAT?

BUT YOU USED TO SAY THE EXACT SAME THI...

BEEP

HUH? WAIT UP!

YASU?!

BEEP

IT'S SUPPOSED TO BE STRAIGHT AHEAD.

LET'S SEE...

WE'RE HERE!

LOOK!

WHAT ARE WE GOING TO FIND AMONG ALL THESE BUILDINGS?

T-THIS IS IT!

T-TOTALLY FINE!

WE'RE GOING IN THE RIGHT DIRECTION!

EVERYTHING OKAY, MAYA?

SUGIHARA-SENPAI, DO YOU KNOW ABOUT DEAF SPORTS?

UM, LIKE GAMES FOR PEOPLE WHO CAN'T HEAR?

EXACTLY. THIS IS MY FIRST TIME TRYING IT OUT, TOO.

THERE WAS A LINK ON THE SIG-N BLOG.

IT'S A FUTSAL TEAM PUT TOGETHER BY MEMBERS OF A SIGN LANGUAGE CLUB.

A CHANCE TO PRACTICE SIGNING WHILE PLAYING SPORTS.

HUH.

DEAF FUTSAL TEAM
SIGN LANGUAGE CLUB
フットサル
サークル

i hear
the
sunspot
limit

i hear the sunspot
limit

THWAP!

SKKT!

SKT

SKT

KICK!

I ASKED AROUND WHEREVER I COULD AND FINALLY MANAGED TO PULL TOGETHER A TE...

PING!

SLAM!

HUH?! ALREADY?! YOU'VE BARELY EVEN STARTED, RYU-CHAN!

SWAP IN FOR ME. I'M TIRED.

A-ARE YOU OKAY?!

MY HEAD!!

URR-RGH!

OWWWW

HEY.

UH...?

?

I TAKE IT YOU DON'T REMEMBER ME?

UM.

THANKS FOR THE OTHER DAY.

WHY DO YOU WANT TO BE A LABOR SPECIALIST?

HUH?

UM...

WELL...

I GUESS

I'VE ALWAYS LOOKED UP TO THE IDEA OF WORKING.

I'VE NEVER HAD A JOB. NOT EVEN PART TIME.

SO I DIDN'T EVEN TRY TO GET ONE.

FIGURED MY HEARING WOULD MAKE ME A HASSLE.

AROUND THAT TIME, I MET SOMEONE WHO WAS THE COMPLETE OPPOSITE OF ME.

KER-CHAK

DO I EVEN WANT TO GO AGAIN?

SEE YOU LATER!

HEY, MOM. I'M HOME.

...

I WAS JUST HERE TALKING BUSINESS WITH YOUR MOTHER.

AH, THANKS.

QUITE THE CHARMER.

IT'S BEEN A WHILE.

HAND-SOME AS EVER, I SEE.

OH, THERE YOU ARE, KOHEI!

HEY THERE!

ENJOYED SOME OF HER EXQUISITE FOOD, AND IT GOT LATE BEFORE WE KNEW IT.

BUSINESS?

OH.

HI, SUZUKI-SAN.

HEE HEE!

YOUR MOM'S GOING TO BE ON TV!

WAIT UNTIL YOU HEAR THIS, KOHEI!

WELL, THAT, TOO, BUT...

ANOTHER BOOK DEAL?

HEH HEH HEH.

...

SUGIHARA-SAN, I HAD NO IDEA YOU WERE SUCH AN ASPIRING STAR.

AHAHA

THIS IS SO EXCITING!

TWIRL TWIRL

OH, WHAT TO WEAR, WHAT TO WEAR!

TWIRL

RUSTLE RUSTLE!

HEY!

BE SURE TO WATCH YOUR STEP!

WHOO!

AHAHA!

NOT TO MENTION, THAT GROUP ENDED UP GROWING THE CLOSEST OF ALL.

WHAT'S THE BIG IDEA?

HEHE. I'M IN CHARGE OF PHOTOS FOR THE DAY.

?!

FLASH!

CHIBA-SAN, OVER HERE!

REALLY? THAT'S NOT HOW I SEE IT.

THEY'RE JUST HUMORING HIM. THEY DON'T TAKE HIM SERIOUSLY.

MOST OF ALL, HE'S JUST GOOD AT UNDERSTANDING PEOPLE.

HE SEEMS SILLY AND IMPULSIVE AT FIRST GLANCE, BUT HE'S

ACTUALLY QUITE PERCEPTIVE AND SENSITIVE TO OTHERS.

NOT LIKE EMPATHY'S ANY RARE GIFT, BUT

IT'S NOT TOO COMMON TO FIND PEOPLE WHO PICK UP SO EASILY ON WHAT OTHERS WANT AND WHAT THEY'RE GOING THROUGH.

GUESS YOU'D SAY HE'S GOT HIS OWN SET OF TALENTS. WONDER HOW YOU RAISE SOMEONE TO BE LIKE THAT.

YOU KNOW, HE'S KINDA

LIKE YOU USED TO BE, NOT SO LONG AGO.

DON'T TELL ME YOU DIDN'T HAVE THE SAME THOUGHT.

WHAT ON EARTH DO WE HAVE IN COMMON?!

WHAT.

DUNNO WHAT YOU'RE TALKING ABOUT.

THAT'S WHY YOU'RE SO STRICT WITH HIM, ISN'T IT? OR MAYBE I SHOULD SAY

OVERPRO-TECTIVE OF HIM?

YEOUCH!!

AHAHA!

WOW!

WHOO!

i hear
the
sunspot
limit

i hear the sunspot
limit

I GUESS

I WAS IN THIRD GRADE OR SO.

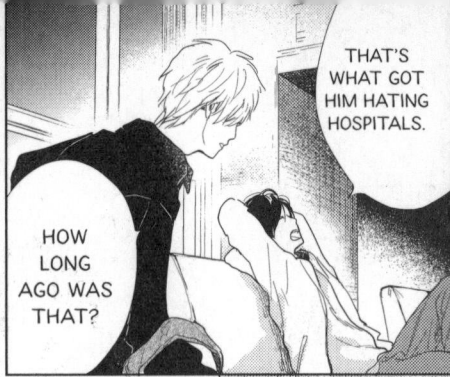

THAT'S WHAT GOT HIM HATING HOSPITALS.

HOW LONG AGO WAS THAT?

WISH I COULD HAVE SOME OF HER OHAGI RIGHT ABOUT NOW.

MAN, THAT BRINGS BACK MEMORIES.

GRANDMA WAS REAL NICE TO ME. AND HER COOKING WAS THE BEST.

WHENEVER I WENT OVER, SHE'D ALWAYS HAVE A BUNCH OF TREATS.

OH!

WHAT AM I DOING?!!

I DIDN'T MEAN TO BORE YOU WITH A BUNCH OF OLD MEMORIES!

HM?

I LOVED HER A LOT.

BUT I DIDN'T KNOW MUCH ABOUT WHAT WAS GOING ON.

AND I MUST HAVE CAUGHT THEM AS THEY WERE WORKING OUT THE DETAILS.

LOOKING BACK, THE DIVORCE HAD PROBABLY ALREADY BEEN FINALIZED.

I WAS JUST THINKING WHAT A LONG TIME IT'D BEEN SINCE I LAST SAW GRANDPA.

HE'S GOT TWO KIDS, STILL IN KINDERGARTEN.

THERE'S NO WAY I CAN LOOK AFTER THEM AND TAKE CARE OF TAICHI.

PRETTY SOON I REALIZED THEY WERE TALKING ABOUT ME.

AND YOU CALL YOURSELF A MOTHER.

ARE YOU LISTENING? I SAID I CAN'T DO IT.

...

... MIT...

...!

...

HFF.

HEH.

GRIN!

TAICHI.

I'M... FINE... NOW.

SORRY, KOHEI.

SNIFF!

SNIFF!

I DIDN'T MEAN TO LET YOU SEE ME LIKE THIS.

i hear
the
sunspot
limit

i hear the sunspot
limit

DONE IT WITH A GUY BEFORE, EITHER.

I'VE NEVER

I DUNNO HOW SMOOTHLY THINGS WILL GO THE FIRST TIME, BUT...

GAH!

ONE. TWO.

?!

KO...

URGHHHH!

HE'S ALREADY GOT ME!

A THUMB WAR.

PRESS

PRESS

PRESS

THREE.

FOUR.

HUH?! WHAT'S GOING ON?!

I DECLARE

ARE WE HAVING A THUMB WAR?!

FREE!

AHA!!!!

10!

PRESS

NGHHH–HH!!

2 3 4 5 6 7 8 9 ...

PRESS

PRESS

PRESS!

AHHHHHHHH!!

GOTCHA AGAIN. ONE.

YOU GOTTA GIVE ME ONE MORE...

HANG ON! ONE MORE ROUND!

HAHA!

I CAN'T BELIEVE I LOST!!

DAMMIT!!

NO FREAKIN' WAY.

GONNA BE IN TO WORK TOMORROW?

GOOD. GLAD TO HEAR IT.

HE HAS TO STAY IN THE HOSPITAL, BUT IT'S NO BIG DEAL.

MY GRANDPA'S TOTALLY FINE!

Y-YEAH! I'LL BE THERE!

SORRY I MISSED YOUR MESSAGE.

TAKE A HALF DAY AND REST UP.

DON'T NEED YOU HERE IN THE MORNING. WE'LL JUST BE UNPACKING FROM THE RETREAT.

HUH?

ALRIGHT. BUT TAKE THE MORNING OFF.

... I DO.

THANK YOU.

SEE YOU IN THE AF-TERNOON!

GOT THAT?

BUT...

YOU'RE GONNA STOP BY THE HOSPITAL ANYWAY, RIGHT? YOU CAN USE THE TIME.

USED TO GO ON AND ON ABOUT HOW HE PISSED YOU OFF.

WHAT?

YOU TWO ARE PRETTY CLOSE THESE DAYS.

BOUGHT ME DINNER AND STUFF.

YEAH, WELL, HE STILL DOES, BUT

OH.

HE'S NOT THAT BAD OF A GUY.

I'VE BEEN READING THE BLOG.

I KNOW.

HAVE I TOLD YOU YET? WE HELD IT AT KAWAGUCHI LAKE.

ALL KINDS OF STUFF HAPPENED.

OH, THE RETREAT! THINGS WERE SO HECTIC THERE!

I SAW THE PICTURES.

THE ONE YOUR COMPANY WRITES.

THE BLOG?

YOU SHOT OFF SOME FIREWORKS THE LAST DAY, RIGHT?

OH, YEAH! ABOUT THAT!

YOU'VE HAD A LONG DAY TODAY. I'M SURE YOU'RE TIRED.

LET'S JUST GET SOME SLEEP.

RIGHT

TAICHI?

IF YOU'RE GOING IN TOMORROW, YOU SHOULD GET SOME SLEEP.

... OKAY.

... OULD
GO FOR
SOME...

CREEAAAK

MUST'VE BEEN MY IMAGINATION.

P-TMP

YEAH!

WHOO!

YOU ALWAYS PRACTICE HERE?

NICE TO SEE YOU AGAIN.

CRUNCH

UM, NO! THAT'S...

LEMME TAKE A PICTURE TO SEND OUT.

INCH

INCH

JUST HOLD UP!

YOU'RE A HANDSOME GUY. PRETTY SURE YOU CAN GET ANYONE YOU WANT.

HUH? WHAT?

EXCUSE ME?

SO YOU'RE IN A RELATIONSHIP?

SORRY. THERE'S ALREADY SOMEONE I LIKE.

"SORT OF"?

THIS IS REALLY EMBAR-RASSING.

BLUSH!

SORT OF.

IF MY HEARING GETS ANY WORSE

I'M WORRIED I WON'T BE ABLE TO HELP THE PERSON I LOVE WHEN IT'S NEEDED MOST.

THAT I MIGHT NOT BE GOOD ENOUGH.

OOPS. SORRY.

THAT WAS PROBABLY HARD TO FOLLO...

SKKT!

SKKT!

THE COURT IS FOR EVERYONE. LET'S KEEP IT CLEAN.

共用コートを
きれいに
使いましょう

KINDA PISSES ME OFF.

SORRY. WHAT WAS THAT?

HIS SIGNING JUST GOT WAY FASTER.

HUH? UM...

YEAH, BUT THE PERSON I LIKE

ISN'T DEAF, AND...

WHAT IS THIS FEELING?

HUH?

IS IT BECAUSE YOU DON'T WANT TO BECOME A PERSON WHO i DOESN'T?

TH-THAT'S NOT...

"ONLY LASTED FOR A MOMENT."

KIIII

"HE'S RIGHT, YOU KNOW."

I WAS ONLY ON THE OTHER SIDE FOR A MOMENT.

I THOUGHT I
WAS READY

P-TMP

IF IT REALLY CAME TO THAT...

i hear
the
sunspot
limit

WAY BACK WHEN

M–MY...

OHAGI!!

SNIFF! SNIFF!

SNIFF!

YOU'RE HANDING THOSE OVER LIKE IT'S THE END OF THE WORLD.

QUIET DOWN ALREADY, YOU LITTLE TWERP!

REALLY?!! GRANDMA, YOU'RE THE BEST!!

THERE'S STILL PLENTY MORE OHAGI FOR YOU.

DON'T YOU WORRY.

GOODNESS, YOU'RE A RIOT, TAICHI!

MY, IT'S BEEN YEARS SINCE I MADE MY WAY FROM THIS WORLD.

BUT HE'S GROWN UP LIVELY AS EVER, BOTH GOOD AND TRUE.

AFTER THAT, TAICHI'S TROUBLEMAKING DIED DOWN.

EXCEPT FOR ONE THING.

HURRY UP AND GIVE US YOUR WALLET!

COME O...

!

KA-POW!

GOODNESS ME! あらあら #あらあら

SAGAWA FAMILY GRAVE
佐川家之墓

Y'KNOW, HALF THE REASON HE'S LIKE THIS IS BECAUSE OF YOU.

HE INSISTS ON GIVING A GOOD WHOOPING TO ANYONE BEING MEAN.

SEEMS HE'S BECOME REAL QUICK TO GET INTO A FIGHT.

WH-WHAT GIVES?! WHO THE HELL ARE YOU?!

SHUT IT! YOU THINK YOU CAN JUST MUG SOME POOR KID?!

だ

BRING IT ON!

Fin

NO PROB!

TOTALLY ON BOARD

LET'S

DO IT!

UM, I DON'T THINK THIS WILL WORK AS A STANDALONE. IS THERE ANY WAY WE CAN MAKE THIS A SERIES?

IT WASN'T GOING TO FIT NEATLY INTO ONE VOLUME LIKE THE OTHERS. I APPROACHED MY PUBLISHER APPREHENSIVELY.

I REALIZED A FUNDAMENTAL PROBLEM.

THIS IS WAY TOO BIG FOR ONE BOOK.

ON SKETCHING OUT THE PLOT FOR LIMIT

IT GOT TO YOU THAT MUCH?!

LISTEN. I HAD TO CLOSE MY BROWSER DOWN WHILE READING SO I HAD A MOMENT TO COMPOSE MYSELF.

ON SUBMITTING THE STORYBOARD FOR VOLUME 5.

MY EDITOR WAS SO HAPPY TO SEE THEIR RELATIONSHIP MOVE FORWARD.

IT'S REALLY KIND OF YOU!

THE TWO OF THEM— THEY'RE DATING!

SO I SUBMITTED THE STORYBOARD FOR VOLUME 1.

'CAUSE THEIR RELATIONSHIP HADN'T GONE ANYWHERE UP UNTIL NOW.

THANKS FOR YOUR PATIENCE.

I HOPE I'LL SEE YOU AGAIN NEXT VOLUME.

AND DETERMINED TO SEE IT THROUGH TO THE END.

I'M OVERJOYED TO KEEP TELLING THE STORY OF THESE TWO.

GRIN!

WITH AT LEAST THE FIRST VOLUME OF LIMIT SAFELY OUT.

SO HERE WE ARE.

I Hear the Sunspot: Limit Vol. 1
(original Japanese title: Hidamari Ga Kikoeru: Limit Vol. 1)
Copyright © 2017 Yuki Fumino
English translation rights arranged with France Shoin
through Japan UNI Agency, Inc., Tokyo

ISBN: 978-1-64273-004-3

Written and illustrated by Yuki Fumino
Translated by Stephen Kohler
English Edition Published by One Peace Books 2018

Printed in Canada
3 4 5 6 7 8 9 10

One Peace Books
43-32 22nd Street STE 204 Long Island City New York 11101
www.onepeacebooks.com

Sam thought he felt icy-cold fingers touch the tip of his nose, then brush slo-o-owly across his face. Or was it just that weird breeze again?

"I smell chocolate . . ." Belinda whispered. "Don't you?"

"No," said Robert. "But I think I see . . . *whoa!*"

Out of the blackness, something white floated toward the kids.

At first it looked like a glowing plume of smoke. But as it floated nearer, it began to change shape.

It got longer and thinner at one end.

It got rounder at the other end.

"It's beginning to look sort of . . . sort of like a *person!*" Belinda gasped.

The ghost
Who Ate
Chocolate

The ghost Who Ate Chocolate

by Susan Saunders
illustrated by Jane Manning

HarperTrophy
A Division of HarperCollinsPublishers

For Tristan

The Ghost Who Ate Chocolate
Text copyright © 1996 by Susan Saunders
Illustrations copyright © 1996 by Jane Manning
Printed in the U.S.A. All rights reserved.

Library of Congress Cataloging-in-Publication Data
Saunders, Susan.
  The ghost who ate chocolate / by Susan Saunders ; illustrated by Jane
Manning.
      p.   cm. — (The Black Cat Club ; #1)
  Summary: When nine-year-old Sam Quirk and several friends decide to form a
ghost-hunting club, their first adventure leads them from the cemetery to the
town's new library.
    ISBN 0-06-442035-3 (pbk.)
    [1. Ghosts—Fiction.]   I. Manning, Jane K., ill.   II. Title.   III. Series: Saunders,
Susan. Black Cat Club ; #1.
PZ7.S2577Gh   1996   96-14566
[Fic]—dc20   CIP
                                                                                    AC

Typography by Darcy Soper
1   2   3   4   5   6   7   8   9   10
❖
First Edition

Don't miss these other Black Cat Club books:

#2: The Haunted Skateboard

and coming soon:

#3: The Curse of the Cat Mummy

Chapter One

Sometimes Sam Quirk and Robert Sullivan were best friends, and sometimes they weren't.

Right now, they weren't. They were arguing about ghosts on Sam's front porch. Belinda Marks and her little brother, Andrew, were there too.

"But there *are* ghosts. Don't you ever read the newspapers at the supermarket?" Sam was saying. "There are ghosts in old houses. And shipwreck ghosts that pull swimmers straight down—and drown them! And ghosts in crashed cars, with bloody stumps where arms and legs used to be. Why shouldn't we have ghosts right here in Maplewood?"

"Give me a break! There are no such things in Maplewood, or anywhere else," Robert said.

"Are too," said Sam.

Okay, he wasn't one hundred percent sure that ghosts were real. But he

wasn't one hundred percent sure they weren't, either.

"Are not," Robert said.

"We've probably got witches and vampires, too!" said Sam.

"Vampires—wow!" said Andrew. He peered up at the sky as if a vampire might swoop down on him any second.

"You can't really believe in that junk!" Robert said to Sam.

Robert was really starting to bug him.

"I'll prove to you there are ghosts. I'm starting a club," Sam announced. "A ghost-hunting club. And I'm calling it . . . calling it . . ." He thought hard.

Then he spotted Belinda's fat black cat, Mittens, slinking under the fence toward the Markses' house.

"I'm calling it the Black Cat Club!" Sam said.

"Cool!" said Belinda.

"It sounds scary," said Andrew.

"It sounds dumb," Robert said.

"You're just mad because you didn't think of it," Sam said to Robert.

Robert snorted. "I have better ways to spend my summer vacation than looking for something that *isn't even there*."

"Suit yourself," said Sam with a shrug. "What about you, Belinda?"

"Let's go for it," said Belinda. She was willing to try anything at least once.

"What are we waiting for, then? Let's start with the old cemetery," Sam said. "There has to be a ghost or two hanging around Shady Rest."

"I'll grab my bike," said Belinda.

"Me too," said Andrew.

"I don't know, Andrew. Things could get pretty creepy," Sam warned him.

After all, Andrew was barely seven—two years younger than they were.

"You're too little," Belinda said to her brother. "I know you, Andrew—the first ghost we meet, you'll be whining and crying to go home. And I won't take you!"

"I'm not scared of ghosts or vampires or werewolves! And if you guys don't let me in the club, I'll . . . I'll tell Mom you're messing around in cemeteries!" Andrew said to his sister. "I'll tell her that a giant headless ghost with blood dripping from his neck shot up out of the ground. And that he chased you and tried to drag you back to his smelly old grave and—"

Belinda covered her ears. "He never stops talking!" she said to Sam and Robert.

"Okay, okay!" she added to Andrew. "You can come with us if you promise not to say another word."

Andrew clapped his hand over his mouth and nodded.

He and Belinda hurried through Sam's back gate to get their bikes.

That left Sam and Robert alone.

They frowned at each other.

Then Robert rolled his eyes and sighed.

"So . . . I guess I'll see you later," Sam said to Robert.

"Yeah, sure," Robert said. "Later."

He slouched across the lawn toward his own house.

Chapter Two

Sam, Belinda, and Andrew pedaled their bikes down Mill Lane and turned left on State Street.

Andrew had already forgotten about his promise to keep quiet.

"We need caps that say 'Black Cat Club' on the front," he said. Andrew always wore a cap.

"I have a feeling we're going to be famous!" he went on. "They'll probably make action toys of us, and a movie about us, and—"

"*Cut!*" Belinda yelled at Andrew. "That means *'Enough already!'* in movie talk."

They were coming to the end of State Street.

"There's the entrance to Shady Rest," said Sam.

The three of them stopped pedaling at the sight of the huge, rusty iron gates standing half open. Across the top of the gates was an arch with the words A LITTLE SLEEP, A LITTLE SLUMBER welded to it.

"What does that mean?" Andrew asked.

"It means that people aren't really dead when they die. They're just sleeping," his sister answered.

"And what if they wake up?" Andrew asked.

"Then they're ghosts!" Sam replied, as though it wouldn't matter to him one bit if the dead did wake up. But a cool, clammy breeze tickled his neck, and the hair on his arms stood straight up.

Sam hunched up his shoulders. He could do without so many dumb questions from Andrew!

"Creepy . . ." Andrew murmured.

Shady Rest *was* a creepy place, even on a sunny afternoon. There were no people around. Or no living ones, at least.

The faded brick path that wound through the cemetery was slippery with green moss. On either side of the path, crumbling tombstones leaned this way and that, like broken, crooked teeth.

Most of them were flat, blackish stones. But a little farther along, a chalk-white marble angel loomed over the path.

Half of the angel's head was missing. The smile on its lips looked more like a snarl.

Sam swallowed hard. "Well," he said, "let's check it out."

Sam, Belinda, and Andrew pedaled slowly through the rusting gates of Shady Rest Cemetery.

"Maybe we're here at the wrong time," Andrew said in a shaky voice. "Ghosts only come out at night, don't they?"

Like the kid really wants to be here at

night! Sam thought. Out loud he said, "Ghosts come out anytime they feel like it."

And suddenly the day seemed darker.

Sam gazed past the leafless, twisted branches of a dying tree, toward the spot where the sun had been. Now the sky was an unfriendly, flat gray.

"It's clouding up," said Belinda.

Andrew shivered. "Isn't it almost time for dinner?" he asked.

"Not even close," said Belinda. "Andrew, you'd better not chicken out. Because I'm not taking you home until I'm good and ready." And she pedaled ahead.

"I wasn't being a chicken," Andrew muttered. "I was just . . . hungry."

The dates on the tombstones slipped farther and farther back in time as Sam, Belinda, and Andrew moved farther away from the cemetery gates.

Belinda read the numbers carved on the stones while her bike bumped along the path: "1875 . . . 1851 . . . 1843 . . ."

Sam joined in: "1822 ... 1816 ... Wow— 1797! That's two hundred years old!"

. . . *Or two hundred years dead,* he added to himself.

For the first time, Sam wondered what they would do if they actually found a ghost. He didn't have a clue.

The older the tombstones, the smaller and harder to read they became. The names and dates carved into them had been worn down for centuries by the weather.

"Hey, a little baby tombstone!" Andrew said, stopping beside a tiny square of black rock not much larger than a comic book.

Sam and Belinda pulled their bikes over to take a closer look.

"It *was* a baby," said Belinda, tracing the dates on the rock with her fingertips. "'Jonas Jackson, born and died January 1782,'" she read. "Poor little guy—he barely lived at all."

They stood quietly for a moment,

staring down at the baby's grave.

"How did he die?" Andrew wondered aloud.

"Maybe there wasn't enough food," said Belinda. "Or maybe he had measles.

Babies could die of measles in the old days."

Sam was thinking about a baby ghost. Would it cry all the time?

Then *cra-a-ack!* A bolt of lightning split the sky above them.

Rain started falling in sheets.

"We're going to get soaked!" said Belinda.

"There's a shed over there!" Sam said, pointing.

They grabbed their bikes and pushed them between tombstones until they reached a little stone house with a peaked roof.

Belinda pulled open the splintery wooden door and peered inside.

"It's empty," she said. "And dry."

But all three of them hung back. What kind of house would be in a cemetery?

"It looks spooky," Andrew said.

Then another lightning bolt tore through the clouds.

Dropping their bikes, they dashed

through the doorway into a small room with a low ceiling.

There were no windows in the shed. The only light came from the open doorway. But once Sam's eyes got used to the gloom, he could see the outlines of neat squares cut into the stone walls.

"It looks like there are drawers in the walls," Andrew said, wiping his wet face on his T-shirt.

If they *were* drawers, Sam was getting a creepy feeling about what they might hold. After all, this *was* a cemetery.

He cleared his throat. "Arr-hmm . . . I think maybe people are buried in the walls here," Sam said.

"In other words, Andrew, we're standing in a tomb, just inches away from the moldy skeletons of a bunch of dead people," Belinda said quietly.

"*Yikes!*" Andrew yelped, and leaped toward the door.

"No you don't!" Belinda said, grabbing his arm. "You're staying in here,

Andrew. If you get wet and catch a cold, Mom will blame me!"

Before Andrew could open his mouth to argue, the wooden door to the outside slammed shut.

Chapter Three

"B-B-Belindaaa!" Andrew wailed.

"Stop it, Andrew!" Belinda said sternly. "I'm right here. The wind blew the door closed."

"It was just the wind," Sam repeated, wishing he really meant it.

With the door shut, it was pitch-dark inside the tomb—so dark that Sam couldn't see his fingers even when he waved them in front of his face.

If he couldn't see his own hand, what else wasn't he seeing? There must have been at least twenty squares carved into the walls. That meant twenty dead bodies—and twenty ghosts.

"It could get awfully crowded in here!" Sam mumbled.

He stepped forward into the blackness, feeling his way along a wall toward the doorway. First he felt smooth stone. Then his hand passed over those squares—squares that marked dead bodies. And finally he touched dry, splintery wood.

"Here's the door," Sam said. "I'll just push it open . . ."

He pushed hard.

The door moved an inch or two. Then it slammed shut again.

"Sam?" Belinda said in the darkness. "What's the matter?"

"Hee-ya!" Sam screamed, and gave the door his best karate kick. The door didn't budge!

Had a tombstone tipped over in the rain and fallen against it?

Or something much worse?

"G-ghosts are s-stronger than any living human being," Andrew stuttered. "A monster ghost will come in here—s-slip right through the door—and r-rip our heads off because we can't run away!"

"Andrew, be quiet!" Belinda said. Then she called out, "I'll help you, Sam."

Sam felt her right arm next to his left as she put both of her hands on the wooden door. What if this didn't work either?

Weeks from now somebody would find his body, and Belinda's, and Andrew's, the life squashed out of them by a hideous fiend. . . .

Stop it! Sam said to himself.

Belinda counted: "One . . . two . . . three!"

On *three,* she and Sam pushed with all their might.

The door held for a split second. Then it swung open all the way, and light streamed into the tomb.

The rain had stopped, and the sun was shining through the clouds.

There was a splash, as though something had fallen into a puddle.

Then Sam heard somebody laughing.

And it sure wasn't a ghostly laugh. It was a laugh Sam had heard a thousand times before.

First he was relieved. Then he was angry!

"Very funny, Robert Sullivan!" Sam shouted as he and Belinda and Andrew piled through the door.

Sure enough, there was Robert, soaking wet, but very pleased with himself.

"I really got you going, didn't I?" Robert said. "I'll bet you thought I was some mean old ghost. You guys look totally freaked out!"

"In your dreams!" said Sam. He was feeling much calmer in the sunshine.

"If we were afraid of anything . . ." Belinda began.

". . . which we weren't," Sam added.

". . . it was that the wind had blown the door closed, and that we might be trapped for days!" Belinda finished, glaring at Robert.

"So what are you doing here, any-way?" Sam asked him.

"I heard about a ghost," Robert said.

"Stop fooling around, okay?" said Sam. Robert never knew when to quit.

"No, I really *did* hear about a ghost," Robert said. He shrugged. "Not that I believe in ghosts. But I thought we could look into it."

"We?" said Belinda. "Just who do you mean by *we*?"

"And where is this so-called ghost supposed to hang out?" Sam asked.

He expected Robert to say an empty house, or maybe Greenlawn, the other cemetery in town.

But Robert said, "At the new library."

"Oh, sure!" said Sam. "Ghosts always head straight for brand-new libraries!"

"The library has been open for about two weeks total, Robert," Belinda said. "No way is that long enough for it to have its very own ghost!"

But suddenly Andrew spoke up: "Hey, I've heard of that library ghost. Greg Logan told me about it at Cub Scouts. His brother said maybe it's some kind of poker . . . pokerguy."

"Poltergeist," said Sam. "That's a ghost that makes noises and throws things."

"So why didn't you say something about it earlier, Andrew?" Belinda wanted to know.

"Because I forgot!" Andrew said to Belinda. "I'm only seven!"

"Listen to me!" Robert said. "I went to the library to return a video. And a bunch of kids were talking about weird sounds, like bells ringing. And the lights turning off and on by themselves, and other strange stuff too. None of it ever happens when grown-ups are around."

"Some kid is playing a dumb joke," said Sam.

"Probably," Robert agreed. "But the Black Cat Club should look into anything that might be about ghosts, right?"

Sam had a strong feeling that Robert was trying to worm his way into the club.

"That's what you said, Sam," Robert went on. "The whole thing was your dumb idea."

"I guess this *could* be our first case," Belinda said. "Like a practice run. What about it, Sam?"

"Well . . . okay," said Sam.

"But I was hoping for something a little spookier than a ghost in a *library*!" said Belinda.

Chapter Four

The Maplewood Free Library wasn't far from Shady Rest Cemetery. It took the four of them about ten minutes to get there. They shoved their bikes into the shiny rack beside the bright-red front door.

This was Sam's first visit to the new library. He thought nothing could have looked less like a haunted building. The windowpanes gleamed. There was a strong smell of fresh paint. There wasn't a single cobweb to be seen.

"Follow me!" Robert said.

He's taking over already! Sam thought as Robert led them down the stairs. It was starting to make him angry.

The reading room was big and airy. It had lemon-yellow walls and wide windows high above the bookshelves. Kids were sitting at round tables in the middle of the room. They were reading, or messing with computers. Even Andrew would have had a hard time imagining anything spooky happening here.

"I think those bells rang in the back room," Robert said.

He led them down a long hallway with the boys' and girls' bathrooms on either side of it. A water fountain stood at the far end.

Next to the fountain was the door to a small green room without any windows. Rows of floor-to-ceiling bookcases filled most of the space. There was a kid-size desk and chair at the near end of each bookcase.

"Not many places for a big bad ghost to hang out," said Robert.

Sam thought about the tiny tombstone at Shady Rest. *A little baby ghost wouldn't need much space,* he said to himself.

"Now what?" Belinda asked.

Robert shrugged. "You guys are the ghost patrol."

"Well, I guess we'll sit down at these desks and wait for something to happen," said Sam.

He was sure that Robert was counting on *nothing* happening.

The small green room was warm and stuffy. It was hard to stay wide awake.

Soon Andrew's head drooped forward until it rested on his desk.

Robert yawned loudly. "Why don't we give up this ghost idea and turn the Black Cat Club into a skateboarding club?" he said. "Or a biking club? Something fun!"

Suddenly the lights in the room flicked off, and then on again.

"What was that?" Andrew squeaked, sitting bolt upright.

"A brown-out. Too many computers in the reading room for the wiring or something," Robert guessed. "It sure wasn't a ghost."

"I'm about to fall asleep in here," Belinda said.

"Let's find some joke books," Robert suggested.

Belinda and Robert started flipping through books on one of the shelves.

Then, two bookcases away, an entire row of books crashed to the floor.

Everybody jumped.

Sam stood up so fast that his chair flipped over.

"That didn't have anything to do with the computers in the reading room," he said.

Belinda looked startled. Andrew didn't seem to know whether to run out of the green room or crawl under his desk.

Even Robert blinked a few times, surprised. "Who did that?" he called out.

No one answered.

There was an odd buzzing in Sam's ears, almost like static. "Do you guys hear that?" he asked.

"Hear what?" Belinda said.

Sam raced to the far end of the bookcases. Nobody was there.

A librarian hurried into the green room. "This is a library. You must be quiet," she scolded.

Then she spotted the pile of books on the floor. "Who dropped these books?" she wanted to know. Without waiting for an answer, she added, "Pick them up at once, please. And remember—you may use the library only if you follow the rules!"

She marched back down the hall in a huff.

Sam, Belinda, and Robert started putting the books back on the shelf.

"Look at these titles," said Belinda.

" '*Ghosts and Goblins*,' " Sam read out loud. " '*Spooky Doings. Spirits on the Loose*.' "

"Don't you think that's kind of strange?" Belinda said. "Every one of these books is a book about ghosts."

"So what?" said Robert. "Ghosts

aren't the mystery here. The mystery is, what kid is doing this stuff, and why?"

He went on, "We can still call ourselves the Black Cat Club. But I think we should forget about ghosts. Instead, we'll solve real mysteries. This could be our first case."

Sam was not going to let Robert change his club. "We're the Black Cat Club, and we're hunting for ghosts!" he said.

"There's no such thing!" said Robert.

"Here we go again!" said Belinda.

"So why did you bring us here?" Sam asked Robert.

"Guys!" said Belinda.

"I smell chocolate," said Andrew. "Don't you?"

But no one paid attention to him.

"Maybe a kid flicked the light switches when we weren't looking," Belinda said.

But Sam was thinking that the weird stuff at the library wasn't so easy to explain away.

If there was nothing spooky happening, what was that buzzing in his ears that hadn't gone away?

Could it be some kind of . . . ghost radar?

Chapter Five

The next morning Sam, Robert, Belinda, and Andrew met in the Markses' driveway.

"Let's go back to the library," Robert said. "You'll look for"—he rolled his eyes—"*ghosts*. And I'll look for the kid who's really causing trouble."

"Fine," said Sam.

"Fine," said Robert.

"Fine," said Belinda and Andrew.

The same librarian nodded to them when they walked through the reading-room door. This time they read the nameplate on her desk: MRS. GUBBINS.

"I'm glad you're so interested in using the library," Mrs. Gubbins said to them.

"But please try to be a little quieter today."

"We will," said Belinda.

They hurried into the green room. They sat down at the desks, just like they had the day before. This time they didn't have to wait long.

Suddenly they heard a bell ringing. It wasn't a loud clanging. It was more of a faint jingling, like the tiny silver bell on Mittens's collar.

As faint as it was, though, it set Sam's nerves to tingling. And he began to hear that low buzzing in his ears again.

"Where's that ringing noise coming from?" Belinda whispered.

"From the far corner," Robert whispered back.

"Here's the plan," Sam said. "Three of us will cover the aisles between the bookcases. One of us should guard the door—"

"Andrew, you stand by the door," Belinda said. "Yell if you see anybody."

"Okay," Andrew whispered.

The four of them quietly slid their chairs back.

Sam, Belinda, and Robert crept up the aisles between the bookcases.

In his aisle Robert found *Ghosts and Goblins, Spooky Doings,* and *Spirits on the Loose* stacked neatly on the floor.

In her aisle Belinda smelled chocolate.

Hadn't Andrew smelled it the day before?

No ghost is eating a candy bar, Belinda decided. *It's a kid, definitely.*

In his aisle Sam felt an icy breeze curl around his head, even though there were no windows in the green room. And the buzzing in his ears was starting to make him really uncomfortable.

Then Andrew shouted: "Belinda! Sam! Hurry!"

They rushed toward the door.

Andrew was hopping up and down.

"I saw her, I saw her!" he yelled.

"Who?" asked Robert.

"A girl!" Andrew said. "And she was giggling!"

"What did I tell you?" Robert said to the others. "We're dealing with a kid, not a ghost."

Sam felt strangely let down. Did this mean his radar didn't work?

"Let's get her!" Belinda said.

They raced down the hall toward the reading room.

There were only three kids sitting at the tables—two girls and a boy.

"Is she in here?" Sam asked Andrew.

Andrew shook his head. "No."

"Bummer! She already left the library," Robert said.

"I don't think there was time," Sam said.

"Shhh!" hissed Mrs. Gubbins, frowning at them.

"We'll check the bathrooms," Belinda whispered.

She looked in the girls' bathroom.

Sam, Robert, and Andrew checked the boys' bathroom. Just in case.

"Nobody was in there," Belinda said when they gathered in the hall again.

"But the water was running in both sinks."

"It was in ours, too," said Sam.

"Hey—look at the fountain!" said Andrew.

The water in the fountain was gurgling away, as though an invisible hand was pressing down the button. While they stared at it, the splashing water suddenly stopped.

Robert reached the fountain first. "The button was jammed, that's all," he said, jiggling it up and down a few times.

"Andrew, what did the girl look like?" Belinda asked her little brother.

"She had straight brown hair. And she was dressed kind of funny," he said. "In a long white dress, with lots of crinkles. And funny high-top shoes."

"Andrew, you're describing my witch costume from the Halloween before last!" Belinda said.

"So all we know is, we're looking for a girl," said Robert.

Sam's ears were buzzing again. He didn't say it out loud, but he thought: *What if it's a girl ghost?*

Belinda sighed. "We're not getting anywhere," she said.

"Let's check out a video so the trip won't be a total loss," said Robert. "I think they have *Super Plays at the Super Bowl*."

"What about *Ghostbusters*?" said Sam.

Personally, he thought they could use some professional help.

Chapter Six

On the way home Sam, Belinda, and Robert grilled Andrew about the girl in the green room.

"Was she tall or short?" Robert asked.

"Taller than me," said Andrew.

"You're a shrimp. Everybody is taller than you," his sister pointed out.

"What color hair?" asked Sam.

"I told you—brown," said Andrew.

"Thin or fat?" Robert asked.

"Just regular," said Andrew.

"We're not getting anywhere with this," Robert groaned.

But when they biked back to the library later that afternoon to return their video, they took a close look at the kids in the reading room. Maybe one of them was the mystery girl!

"Six boys. They're out," said Robert.

Which left four girls.

Two of them were blond. The other two had dark hair. But one had a short haircut, and Andrew shook his head about the last one.

"Nope," he said. "The girl I saw was skinnier."

"Let's try the green room again," said Sam.

They had barely sat down when—*crash!*—more books thudded to the floor!

Once again Sam, Robert, and Belinda raced up and down the aisles. Once again they saw nobody—ghostly or otherwise.

But Sam's radar was buzzing like crazy.

Now even Robert was baffled. "How does the girl do it?" he said. "She must pull the books out with strings. Or wires. From the hall maybe. Or the bathroom."

Robert crawled around on his hands and knees, searching for clues under the bookcases. He was still trying to solve a regular mystery.

Belinda kneeled beside the books that had fallen.

"Hey, this is interesting," she said. "All of these books are about the history of Maplewood: '*Maplewood from 1850 to 1950. A History of Maplewood in Pictures. Old Maplewood Families . . .*' "

The last book fell open to a page of photographs of girls in long ruffled dresses and lace-up boots.

"Sam, look at these girls," Belinda said.

"Aren't they dressed sort of like the girl Andrew saw?" Sam asked.

"They are!" said Andrew, peering around his sister. "Crinkled dresses and high-tops."

"Why are you wasting your time on stuff from a zillion years ago?" Robert said, jumping up from the floor. "Maybe we can catch her in the reading room!"

Belinda stuck the book back onto the shelf. They all hurried down the hall.

But Mrs. Gubbins blocked their way into the reading room. "Quiet, please. I'm having a half-hour program for preschoolers," she said sternly.

Behind her a bunch of little kids were cutting out shapes from colored paper.

"Did anybody run through here in the last few minutes?" Robert asked her.

"We don't *run* in this library," said Mrs. Gubbins. "No one came in, and no one went out."

The Black Cat Club walked slowly back down the hall.

"No one in or out? How could that be?" said Robert. Then he answered himself: "Easy. Mrs. Gubbins was helping some kid cut out a triangle or something, and the girl slipped past her."

But just after the four of them stepped back into the green room, the door swung closed behind them. All of the lights clicked off and stayed off. The room was pitch-black!

Sam's ears were buzzing like a handful of angry bees.

"Belinda!" Andrew wailed.

"It's like Shady Rest," Sam whispered.

"Only this time Robert's on the inside with us," Belinda murmured.

"I can't see anything," Robert said.

The others could hear him cracking his knuckles.

A bell tinkled softly.

Sam thought he felt icy-cold fingers touch the tip of his nose, then brush slo-o-owly across his face. Or was it just that weird breeze again?

"I smell chocolate . . ." Belinda whispered. "Don't you?"

"No," said Robert. "But I think I see . . . *whoa!*"

Out of the blackness, something white floated toward the kids.

At first it looked like a glowing plume

of smoke. But as it floated nearer, it began to change shape.

It got longer and thinner at one end.

It got rounder at the other end.

"It's beginning to look sort of . . . sort of like a *person*!" Belinda gasped.

"It's got ha-ha-hands!" Andrew croaked. "Long, skinny fingers! It's reaching out. . . ."

Sam could almost feel clammy white hands circling his neck. . . .

The bell tinkled faster and faster. The Black Cat Club squeezed tighter and tighter together.

Belinda was pressed against Sam's left side. He could smell her strawberry shampoo. Robert was pressed against Sam's right side. Andrew had sunk to the floor. His arms were wrapped around Sam's knees. There wasn't a half inch of space between the four of them.

The glowing white thing floated closer. And closer.

Sam didn't know whether to open his eyes wider or close them altogether.

"No-o-o-o!" Belinda moaned.

Just before the white thing touched them, it floated off to one side and straight through the back wall!

Chapter Seven

As soon as the white shape disappeared, the bell stopped tinkling. And Sam's ghost radar stopped buzzing a warning in his ears.

Then the lights flicked back on in the green room.

"Wh-what *was* that?" Belinda asked. Her cheeks were so pale, she looked almost ghostly herself.

"I don't know. I had my eyes closed," Andrew squeaked from the floor. In fact, his head was still pressed tight against Sam's legs.

Robert didn't say anything. He looked frozen with shock, except for his hands. He was cracking his knuckles again.

"It was some kind of trick, right?" Belinda said to Sam.

"S-some trick!" Sam said. "That thing floated straight through the wall."

"Let's leave this library right now! And never come back," Andrew said, scrambling to his feet.

Then Robert seemed to snap out of it. "You guys got me all worked up!" he complained. "What did we *really* see?"

"A gh-ghost!" said Andrew.

"Wrong!" said Robert. "A little kid might think that. But all we really saw was a puff of white smoke."

What was Robert talking about? That white thing wasn't like any smoke Sam had ever seen. "Just where did the smoke come from, anyway?" he asked Robert.

"Maybe from the air conditioners in the reading room," Robert said. "It could have floated down the hall."

"But the door is closed," Sam pointed out.

"So it floated under the door," said Robert.

"Then it floated right through the back wall?" Belinda said, shivering. "I don't think so!"

"So maybe it didn't go *through* the wall," Robert said. "Maybe it just came apart, the way smoke does after a while."

"What about the door closing by itself, and the lights, and the bell?" Sam said. "You talk about solving mysteries, Robert. But real detectives pay attention to clues."

Sam stared at Robert's hands. The only time he'd seen Robert crack his knuckles so much was when they'd watched *Slasher 3: Out of the Grave* together.

"Those were all tricks!" Robert said. "There has to be somebody—some person—behind all this stuff!"

Sam knew Robert was just as frightened as the rest of them. But maybe if he kept saying they hadn't seen a ghost, there would be nothing for him to be scared of.

"Let's get out of here. I need some air," Belinda said weakly.

"I need to go home," moaned her brother.

The four of them were pulling their bikes out of the rack outside when Sam said, "Wait a second, okay? I want to check out a book."

He was back in a flash, stuffing the book into his saddlebag.

Sam didn't tell the others. But he had checked out one of the first books to end up on the floor of the green room: *Spooky Doings*.

Maybe somebody—or something—had been trying to point the way to the truth!

Chapter Eight

It was getting close to dinnertime that day when the phone rang at Sam's house.

It was Belinda, and she sounded panicky.

"Sam, you have to come right over!" she said in a loud whisper. "Hurry!"

"What's going on?" Sam asked her.

"I can't talk now," Belinda said. "Just come. Quick!"

Sam ran out his front door and across the lawn.

On the other side of the street, Robert was working on his bike in his driveway. "Where are you going so fast?" he called to Sam.

"Belinda's!" Sam said. "Come on!"

Belinda was waiting for them on the front porch.

"I think it followed me home!" she told them, her voice shaking.

"What followed you?" said Sam.

"Whatever that was in the library!" said Belinda.

And Sam realized that his ears were buzzing again.

"No way!" Robert was saying, shaking his head.

"Oh yeah? You'll see what I mean," Belinda said. "Come inside, but be quiet. I haven't told Andrew, because I don't want him to make a fuss in front of Mom and Dad."

They ran up the stairs to the second floor.

"I heard that little bell *in my room,*" Belinda said. "Then I smelled chocolate, just the way I did in the library. And I felt a freezing-cold spot near my window.

"Plus, Mittens is totally freaked out,"

she added as they walked into her bedroom. "Just look at him!"

Belinda's black cat, Mittens, was fat. And lazy. He was usually sleeping.

But Mittens wasn't sleeping now. He

was crouched down in a chair, his huge yellow eyes staring wildly toward the window. The hair along his spine was standing straight up. His tail was whipping back and forth like an angry snake. And he was growling deep in his throat.

"How long has he been acting this way?" Sam asked Belinda.

"Since I got back from the library," she said.

"Maybe it's too much catnip," Robert said.

"I never give Mittens catnip," said Belinda. "It makes him sneeze."

"Where's the cold spot?" Sam asked her.

"Over there, near the window," Belinda said, staying away from it herself.

Sam edged toward the window. Then he said, "Yow! I found it!"

It was a hot afternoon, but right in front of Belinda's window was a shaft of icy air.

"Let's see!" Robert said. He moved to

where Sam was standing and stuck out his hand.

"Yeah, it's colder here," Robert said. "But couldn't it be . . ." He looked around the bedroom for an answer.

"It's not a cold breeze, Robert," Belinda said impatiently. "It's hot outside, remember? And it's not a fan, or a refrigerator."

She reached for something small on her dresser. "I haven't shown you what I found," Belinda said, holding out her hand.

"A dime," said Robert. "Big deal."

"Check out the date on it," Belinda said.

Sam picked up the coin. "Wow— 1899!" he said.

"So it's an *old* dime," said Robert.

"I never saw this dime before. Not until this afternoon," said Belinda. "It just showed up on my windowsill. Do you think that . . . that thing was trying to tell me something?"

"*Thing?*" Robert repeated, as if

Belinda was just being silly.

But Sam saw him grip his right hand with his left. Robert was about to start cracking his knuckles.

"That thing, that white smoke . . ." Belinda said. "Whatever it is!"

"I'd call it a ghost!" said Sam. "Wouldn't you?"

There. He had finally said it out loud!

The three of them were quiet for a second.

Then Robert said, "Ghost? There's no way I'm going to believe in ghosts."

Chapter Nine

It was easy to be certain in the after-noon sunlight.

In the middle of the night, though, things were different.

That night Robert dreamed about a girl.

She had straight dark hair. She was wearing a long white dress and weird black shoes.

It's the girl Andrew saw, Robert said to himself in his dream.

She was zipping here and there around the new library, her feet hardly touching the floor. She dumped all the books out of the shelves. She switched the lights on and off, and made the water fountain shoot a stream all the way to Mrs. Gubbins's desk.

If only Robert could see her face—then he would know who she was.

The girl was having a great time. She was giggling.

The giggling woke Robert up.

He opened his eyes wide. . . .

But he could still hear the giggling.

It was coming from somewhere in his bedroom!

"No-o-o! Go away!" Robert yelled.

He grabbed his bedspread and pulled it over his head. He held on to it as tightly as he could. He also held his breath. Maybe it would turn out to be a dream after all.

Then the bedspread was ripped out of Robert's hands.

The top sheet flew off his bed too.

The smell of chocolate filled the room. It was almost sickening!

Just before he squeezed his eyes shut, he saw his top sheet dancing in the air!

"Le-e-eave me alone!" Robert screamed. He was so scared that he curled into a ball.

"Robert?" his parents called out from their bedroom.

But Robert was too frightened to answer.

A few heartbeats later, Robert's dad was standing beside his bed.

"Are you okay, son?" he asked.

Robert's mom was there too.

"You must have been having a nightmare," she said. "Can you remember what it was about?"

"N-no." Robert was shaking too hard to crack his knuckles.

He finally knew the awful truth.

He hadn't been having a nightmare at all.

The ghost who ate chocolate had come to visit him!

Chapter Ten

When the Black Cat Club met the next morning in Sam's yard, Robert told them the whole story.

"I never saw it," he said. "But I sure heard it. And I saw that sheet dancing in the air. It was horrible!"

"What did you do?" Andrew asked him.

"Once my mom and dad left, I let it have my bedroom! I moved into the guest room. And I didn't close my eyes again!"

Robert's eyes *were* awfully red. He cracked a couple of knuckles.

"For all I know, the ghost came back to my house last night—I sure had some spooky dreams!" said Belinda. "I don't want another visit. Not ever. I've never been so scared in my life, and neither has Mittens. He won't go into my room for anything. And take a look at this."

Belinda stuck her arm out so they could see her watch. The hands were whirling around so fast, they were a total blur!

Sam stared at it, and murmured, "Ghosts are supposed to wreck clocks and watches."

"How would you know?" said Robert. "You've never had a ghost at your house!" Even though he was scared, he was still pushy.

"I know because I checked *Spooky Doings* out of the library yesterday," Sam explained. "I figured the ghost must want us to read it, since it kept dumping the book onto the floor."

"What else did you find out?" Belinda asked.

"An open mind is important in really seeing a ghost," Sam replied.

"Well, my mind is open now!" said Robert.

"Mine too," said Belinda. "But I didn't really *see* anything," she added.

"I think Mittens did," said Sam. "And I know Andrew saw her."

"I did?" Andrew said.

"You know the girl you saw at the library?" Sam said to him.

"The one with long hair and a long dress?" said Andrew.

"Right," said Sam. "I'm pretty sure she's our ghost."

"Cool!" Andrew said proudly. "I saw a ghost." As soon as he thought about it, though, he looked scared.

"But why the library?" Robert asked.

"If ghosts are unhappy, sometimes they hang around places they knew when they were alive," Sam said.

"Which doesn't make sense for a brand-new place," Robert pointed out.

"Hey—what if the library was built on top of where the ghost used to live a long time ago?" Belinda said.

"That could work," said Robert.

"Those books about Maplewood's history might give us some clues!" said Sam.

"What are we waiting for, then?" said Robert. "Let's go back to the library. The sooner she's happy, the sooner I'm happy."

"Me too," said Belinda with a shiver.

"But what if *she's* there?" Andrew whispered. "You know—my ghost."

"You'll be safe if you stay with Mrs. Gubbins. This ghost doesn't show herself to grown-ups," said Belinda.

"Mrs. Gubbins?" Andrew thought about it, and shook his head. "I think I'll stick with you guys."

Chapter Eleven

Mrs. Gubbins was waiting at the door to the children's reading room when the Black Cat Club got to the library.

"Oh, I thought you might be the handyman," she said. "We've been having some trouble in the green room."

"What kind of trouble?" asked Sam.

"The lights in there turn off and on, off and on," said Mrs. Gubbins. "It upsets the children. And I can't seem to make the water stop running in the fountain, either."

The kids looked at each other.

"She's ba-a-ack," Robert murmured.

"Can we go into the green room for a book?" Belinda asked.

"Of course. I just hope the lights will stay on for you," said Mrs. Gubbins.

The four of them squared their shoulders and walked quietly down the hall. Sam was waiting for his ghost radar to kick in, but there wasn't even the hint of a buzz in his ears.

The book the kids chose first was *Maplewood from 1850 to 1950*. Sam opened it to the old map in the middle. "Here's Main Street, and State Street, and Donally Park, and the lake," he said.

"Just like Maplewood now," said Andrew.

The top of the map, though, was empty. FARMLAND was printed across it.

"So this whole side of town—where the library is now—used to be farms," said Belinda.

Sam read the date in a corner of the map. "This was drawn in 1897," he said.

"That's almost the exact same date as the old dime in my bedroom," said Belinda.

She pulled *A History of Maplewood in*

Pictures off the shelf and found the chapter for 1890 to 1900.

Sam, Robert, and Andrew crowded around as Belinda turned the pages.

There were photos of old buildings in downtown Maplewood. There were photos of steam engines, and horses and buggies. There were photos of men in funny round hats and fancy suits, women in long dresses, families posed in front of their houses, and—

"Hey! There she is!" Andrew said suddenly. He was staring at a picture of a big family outside a farmhouse.

A man and a woman sat in wooden chairs, and five children stood around them: two boys and three girls.

"There who is, Andrew?" Belinda asked him.

"The girl I saw yesterday! The one who giggled!" Andrew said. He pointed to the little girl in the front row, standing beside her mother.

A chill ran down Sam's spine, and he

checked his radar again, just in case. But it was still quiet.

"Are you sure, Andrew?" Sam asked.

"Don't kid around," said Robert to Andrew.

"I'm sure!" said Andrew.

"Then I'm sure that's our ghost!" said Sam.

Robert read the line under the picture: " 'The Foster Family.' "

"The Foster family!" boomed a man's voice suddenly. The lights in the green room went off.

"Aaaah!" All four kids screamed at once.

Another ghost? thought Sam. *Why isn't my radar working?*

Then the voice said "Sorry," and the lights in the room clicked back on.

A man in blue overalls, with the name BILL stitched on the chest pocket, stood in the doorway. "I didn't mean to scare you," he said. "I'm just here to fix the lights."

He started unscrewing one of the

switch plates. "I know the Foster family. Or at least I know old Miss Foster," Bill said, talking while he worked. "I do some odd jobs for her every now and then."

"The Fosters who owned a farm?" Sam asked him.

"Yep. In fact, their farm was right around here somewhere," Bill said. He pulled electric wires out of the wall.

"The family sold the land twenty or thirty years ago, though," he went on. "Miss Foster is the only one left."

"Do you think we could talk to her?" asked Belinda.

"She'd enjoy the company," Bill said.

He straightened the wires out. Then he twisted them together again and screwed the switch plate back onto the wall.

He turned the lights off. Then on. Then off and on.

Bill rubbed his nose. "Everything seems okay. I can't understand why these lights haven't been working right," he said.

The Black Cat Club kids looked at each other. They knew the problem had nothing to do with the wiring!

"Can you tell us where Miss Foster lives?" Sam asked Bill.

Chapter Twelve

Miss Foster lived a few streets away from the library. Her house was small and wooden, with a crooked chimney. It was covered with ivy.

"This house looks *ancient*!" said Sam.

But it didn't look any older than Miss Foster herself. She was tiny and stooped. Her hair was snow-white. Her face was a crisscross of fine wrinkles.

But her eyes were a sharp, clear green. And she seemed pleased to see them when she opened her front door.

"What a nice surprise!" she said. "Do I know you?"

"No, you don't. But Bill the handyman thought you might be able to tell us something about Maplewood's history," Belinda said.

"Come right in!" said Miss Foster. "I always enjoy talking about the old days."

On their way through the house, the kids walked past a group of photos on a table. One was an old photograph of a man and a woman sitting on chairs outside a farmhouse. Five children stood around them, two boys and three girls. . . .

Robert jabbed Sam in the ribs. "It's the picture from the book!" he said.

"That's my family," said Miss Foster.

Yes! Sam yelled in his head. Maybe they were finally going to get some answers about their ghost!

"Which one is you?" Andrew wanted to know.

Miss Foster laughed. "I'm old," she said. "But I'm not quite that old. I was born after this photograph was taken."

"Can you tell us who everybody is?" Sam asked her.

"Certainly," said Miss Foster. She

pointed to each of the people in the picture: "The two in the chairs are my mother and father, of course. This is my brother Thomas, my sister Mary, my brother Jasper, my sister Kate . . ."

Miss Foster's finger came to rest on the girl Andrew saw at the library.

"And this was Alice," Miss Foster said.

"Alice?" Belinda repeated, hoping Miss Foster would tell them more.

The old woman nodded, and all of a sudden she looked sad. "Alice died when she was only seven years old, before I ever knew her."

"Just my age," said Andrew quietly.

"The year was 1899," Miss Foster told them.

Belinda gasped. "That's the date on the old dime!" she murmured to Sam and Robert.

"Alice died of a fever. In those days doctors didn't have the medicines they do now," Miss Foster said.

She went on, "Alice was buried on

the farm, but I don't remember exactly where now. My brother Jasper often told me that her ghost never left our house."

"Weren't you scared?" Andrew asked.

Miss Foster smiled. "No, I thought he was teasing me. But maybe he wasn't. Jasper used to make us leave candy out for Alice at night. And in the morning it would be gone."

"*Chocolate* candy?" Belinda asked.

"Why yes, dear, that's right," Miss Foster replied. "Jasper said chocolates were Alice's favorite. She was always begging Mama to make fudge for her. Anyway, even though I never saw Alice myself, I was sorry when the old farmhouse was torn down."

She smiled at the Black Cat Club. "That's where the new Maplewood Library is now—right where our old house used to stand."

"I had a feeling . . ." said Sam.

"When they tore the farmhouse down," Miss Foster added, "I couldn't help worrying that Alice wouldn't have anyplace to go."

Sam, Belinda, Andrew, and Robert were all thinking the same thing: *Don't worry too much. Alice has moved into the Maplewood Library. And she's staying very busy.*

They couldn't say that to a grown-up. Not even if the grown-up was Alice's sister.

Chapter Thirteen

The Black Cat Club talked things over on Sam's front porch.

"If it is Alice Foster causing trouble at the new library . . ." Sam began.

". . . and at my house," Belinda reminded him.

". . . and mine," said Robert, "how do we get her to stop?"

"If she's hanging around because she's not happy, then let's do something to cheer her up," said Sam.

"Why would Alice be unhappy?" Andrew asked.

"Look at it this way, Andrew: Alice's house has been torn down," said Sam. "Her family is gone, all except for Miss Foster."

"And not even Miss Foster, her own sister, knows where Alice's grave is," said Belinda.

"Maybe Alice just wants to be remembered," said Robert. "*I* would."

"Let's get a statue of Alice and stick it on the front lawn at the library!" said Andrew. "Like the soldier in front of the courthouse."

"A statue costs way too much," said Robert. "But how about a sign, to hang in the green room?"

"Like the bronze sign in the hall at school!" Belinda exclaimed. "The one that says 'In memory of Principal Michael Yates, who served at Maplewood Elementary from—' "

"Right!" said Robert.

"I know exactly how we'll pay for it, too," said Belinda. "We'll sell the old dime at the coin shop on Main Street."

"Sometimes old coins are worth a lot," Sam said.

"And it's really Alice's coin, anyway,"

Robert pointed out. "She must have left it on the windowsill."

"I wonder what Alice would want her sign to say?" said Belinda.

Sam said, "How about: 'In memory of Alice Foster' . . . How old did Miss Foster say Alice was when she died?"

"Seven," said Andrew. "My age."

"Which means she was born in 1892," said Robert.

" 'In memory of Alice Foster, 1892 to 1899, who lived on a farm where the library now stands,' " said Sam.

"Good!" said Belinda. "And maybe the sign could also say: 'She will never be forgotten.' "

"You bet she won't! Not if she keeps dumping books on the floor," said Andrew.

"And switching the lights off and on," said Sam.

"What about ripping sheets off of beds?" said Robert. He cracked his knuckles just thinking about it.

Chapter Fourteen

The Black Cat Club sold the 1899 dime for a lot more than ten cents. The owner of the Main Street Coin Shop paid them seventy-five dollars for it. And that was enough to buy a small bronze sign.

The club had these words engraved:

For Alice Foster,
who lived on a farm
where the library now stands.
She died young
but will always be remembered.
1892–1899

"Now comes the hard part," said Belinda. "Getting Mrs. Gubbins to let us hang the sign in the green room."

But Robert handled Mrs. Gubbins. "This sign will make kids want to learn more about Maplewood's history," he told the librarian.

"There are some great books about Maplewood on these shelves," Sam joined in, "with old pictures and maps and other cool stuff from long ago."

"Even Alice's picture is in one of them," said Belinda. She opened the photo book to the Foster family.

"This is Alice," Andrew said, pointing her out to Mrs. Gubbins.

And Mrs. Gubbins surprised them all. "What a wonderful idea!" she said. "Perhaps we'll be able to get a copy of the Foster family photo and hang it up next to your sign."

Mrs. Gubbins went to the supply closet for a hammer and nail. Not five minutes later Alice's sign hung proudly outside the door to the green room.

"Now I'd like a picture for the bulletin board of the four of you next to your lovely sign," Mrs. Gubbins said.

When she left the room to get her camera, Andrew said, "I wonder what Alice thinks about all this."

"We could ask her," said Belinda.

Robert frowned. "I've had enough of Alice Foster for this lifetime," he said.

But Belinda was calling softly: "Alice? Alice? Are you here?"

In a split second the lights in the room flashed off and on, off and on!

"She's here all right," Sam murmured. His ears were buzzing again.

Somehow, though, the thought of a ghost—or at least this ghost—wasn't as scary as it used to be. This was *their* ghost, Alice Foster. A kid.

A breeze ruffled their hair, but this time it was a warmer breeze.

They heard the little bell.

And the smell of chocolate filled the green room.

Mrs. Gubbins came back with her camera. It was the kind that takes a picture and rolls it out right away.

"Those lights weren't flickering again, were they?" Mrs. Gubbins asked, looking worried.

The members of the Black Cat Club shook their heads.

"Get closer together," Mrs. Gubbins told them as she peered through the camera.

"Smile," she said. "And point to your sign. Now stand still. . . ."

The flash went off. Mrs. Gubbins caught the photo as it rolled out of the camera.

Then someone called her from the reading room.

"I'll be right back," she said, handing the photo to Sam.

Belinda, Andrew, and Robert pressed close as the picture grew lighter and clearer.

"You've got your goofy grin on," Belinda said to her little brother.

"The sign shows up really well," said Sam.

"Hey, look at that!" said Robert all of a sudden.

They all stared at the photo as it grew even sharper.

In the doorway to the green room was the outline of a girl!

She wasn't exactly all there. They could sort of see through her to the bookshelves beyond. But she had dark, straight hair with a ribbon in it. She was wearing a long white dress with a sash, and black high-top shoes. . . .

Belinda whispered, "It's Alice!"

Sam added, "She's smiling."

"So let's get out of here while she's still in a good mood!" said Robert.

Sam stuck the photo in the pocket of his jeans. The Black Cat Club hurried through the reading room and out to their bikes.

"What do you think will happen to Alice now?" Andrew asked as they pedaled quickly away.

"Maybe she'll be so pleased with her

sign that she'll stop bothering kids at the library," said Sam.

"And at my house!" said Robert.

"We've done all we can for her," Belinda said.

"I think I'm going to miss her," said Andrew sadly.

They had ridden their bikes a few blocks when Sam suddenly stopped pedaling and coasted. There was buzzing in his ears. Was it his ghost radar?

Then Robert asked Belinda, "Do you hear anything funny?"

Belinda slowed down too. Her eyes widened, and she nodded. "A bell tinkling?"

"I hear it!" Andrew said.

"I smell chocolate!" said Sam.

"It's Alice!" Robert said.

"She's giggling," said Andrew.

"Maybe we can still lose her," Robert whispered. He pedaled harder and harder, until he was bright red in the face. But his bike was barely moving!

"Alice is hanging on to you!" said Sam. His ears were buzzing like a dentist's drill.

"She's hanging on to me, too!" said Belinda, just before her bike stopped dead. And Andrew's. And Sam's.

"What does she want?" Andrew whispered.

"She wants us!" Robert croaked, looking around for a place to hide.

But Sam muttered, "Okay, okay—you win, Alice." He added, "It looks like the Black Cat Club has a new member."

Belinda nodded. "Whether we want her or not."

"Which I don't," said Robert, trying to catch his breath.

"I do—she's just my age!" said Andrew.

"Give or take a hundred years," said Sam Quirk.

Don't miss:

The Black Cat Club #2
The Haunted Skateboard

Sam had never seen Robert ride like this before. He never missed a beat. He never bobbled or shook. Not even his head moved. Back and forth, back and forth, up and down the driveway. It was like watching a wind-up toy. Or a robot . . .

Then Sam saw something creepy. Very creepy.

Maybe it was a trick of the moonlight. Maybe he was just too sleepy. But for a moment, Sam thought he saw the ghostly shape of a boy, standing right behind Robert on the skateboard!

Sam blinked and rubbed his eyes. When he opened them again, the ghost boy had disappeared!